NAVIGATING
THE
PARTNERSHIP
MAZE

NAVIGATING THE PARTNERSHIP MAZE

Creating Alliances That Work

SARAH GERDES

McGraw-Hill

New York   Chicago   San Francisco
Lisbon   London   Madrid   Mexico City
Milan   New Delhi   San Juan   Seoul
Singapore   Sydney   Toronto

The *McGraw·Hill* Companies

Library of Congress Cataloging-in-Publication Data

Gerdes, Sarah.
    Navigating the partnership maze : creating alliances that work / Sarah Gerdes.
      p. cm.
    ISBN 0-07-139823-6 (alk. paper)
    1. Strategic alliances (Business)   I. Title.
    HD69.S8 G465   2002
    658'.044—dc21

                        2002009908

1 2 3 4 5 6 7 8 9 0 AGM/AGM 0 9 8 7 6 5 4 3 2

ISBN 0-07-139823-6

Illustrations by Claudette Iebbianno.

McGraw-Hill books are available at special quantity discounts to use as premiums and sales promotions, or for use in corporate training programs. For more information, please write to the Director of Special Sales, Professional Publishing, McGraw-Hill, Two Penn Plaza, New York, NY 10121-2298. Or contact your local bookstore.

 This book is printed on recycled, acid-free paper containing a minimum of 50% recycled, de-inked fiber.

Contents

Introduction

EVERY YEAR, the Cambridge, Massachusetts, universities of MIT and Harvard host the most prestigious entrepreneurship business plan competition in the United States. Students from both schools compete for a $50,000 prize and the validation of their business plan. Past winners of this event have gone on to form companies, receive funding, and take their firms public. Quite a few companies have been acquired. Four weeks before the 2000 event, I accepted an invitation from the director of entrepreneurship from each school to speak on the subject of strategic partnerships. Why this topic? Because "the lack of a partner strategy" is the primary reason start-up business plans fail to receive funding. Of those that are funded without a partner strategy, many prematurely fail.

A month following this event, I accepted an invitation to speak about partner development at a forum composed of seasoned CEOs. While vastly different in terms of business experience and success, the group of 450 had no more understanding of the partnership development essentials than the business school students. The majority of CEOs said that they had come to the meeting to learn the fundamentals of choosing the right partner, creating the relationships, and making the partnerships successful on a sustainable basis.

That's when the idea for this book was born. If both business novice and expert were struggling with the same questions, what better way to communicate proven strategies than through a partnership development guide?

Partnerships Defined

Partnerships are created in order to achieve better business results than could be accomplished by either partner alone. Partnerships accelerate time to market, lower costs of goods, improve quality, and expedite global expansion. Increased short-term revenue is realized while higher margins and shareholder value are long-term results.

If achieving success through partnership development sounds challenging, let me assure you it's not. Partnership development is just not well *understood*. Cluttered with fancy phrases and shrouded by myths, partnership development is often viewed as a combination of luck and a golden Rolodex. This perception could not be further from the truth. Successful partnerships start in the selection of the right partner. By using a tool I've created, called *AllianceMapping*, you can save yourself many months of effort, as well as thousands of dollars, in pursuit of an incompatible partner. The next step is to follow a partnership development road map, which is consistent across industries and product lines. Behind each process are specific techniques to accelerate the activity and avoid time-consuming sand traps or dead ends.

Unfortunately, few alliance managers, entrepreneurs, and CEOs are prepared for the experience of partnership development. How, for example, would you know why a potential partner has not returned your call? Was it because your proposal was off the mark, or because a product manager averages 400 new voice mails a day? How would you react to learning your potential partner doesn't engage with a "firm of your size" after six months' worth of effort? What happens when you are told that you have been automatically rated, ranked, and placed into an internal "category" without consultation, simply by registering on a potential partner's Web-based partner portal? Each and every example reflects a reality of partnership development in today's environment.

Without understanding the partnership development landscape and the right strategies for success, you will be endlessly frustrated by the lack of movement and results. This book, *Navigating the Partnership Maze*, will walk you through the partnership development life cycle, providing each and every component necessary to create a sustainable, smoothly functioning partnership development team, so that you can achieve greater returns in less time.

The Good, the Bad, and the Ugly:
Partnership Development Statistics

Understanding what a "good" partnership development team can produce is predicated on knowing what "average" teams produce in the way of partnerships. When my company, Business Marketing Group (BMG) was formed, we did some research into other companies' client partnerships development efforts. The good news: we found that companies of *all* sizes were able to create partnerships with and without outside assistance. The bad news came in the form of the time commitment needed to forge such partnerships. We found that it takes companies an average of 18 to 24 months to create a partnership—from the first phone call to realizing the first revenue dollar. Broken down, it takes roughly 4 months to identify the individual responsible for partnership decisions within the appropriate company. Once done, four to six meetings are required before an initial yes decision is made. The statistics got even uglier when we determined the return on investment to be a measly $35,000—far less than the $75,000 annual salary required to retain a good alliance manager. That's a lot of time, money, and meetings without any tangible results!

Exploration and Discovery

Though every industry, client, and partnership has its own particular needs, we started to see some common elements and experiences shared by *all* partnerships. We started to plot a road map—a plan that captured the entire process and charted the milestone elements common in each type of partnership. Further exploration of this road map enabled us to identify the trends, pitfalls, resources, and outcomes associated with different types of partnerships.

Initially, our partnership development road map was used and tested by small companies pursuing partnerships with the largest, most complex firms in the world: Sony, Disney, IBM, Hewlett-Packard, Microsoft, American Express, and Bank of America. Over the years, this same road map has proved viable in over 35 industries, each time by a company seeking a partnership and entrusting their course of actions to a consistent, replicable process.

It was during this time that we made a second and more important discovery: We realized it was possible to remove the guesswork from selecting and validating the best partner. Since successful partnerships rely heavily on the organizations' ability to make the right choices early in the process, we realized a model must exist for reducing the risk and uncertainty associated with choosing the ideal partner.

The result of this analysis was the creation of the AllianceMapping™ model: an easy-to-understand tool that enables us to pinpoint the right type of potential partner for our clients. As our model has gained validation from companies of all sizes in a variety of product and service industries, we have employed it at the forefront of our partnership planning efforts.

The outcome of using AllianceMapping and the partnership development program is noteworthy. By using AllianceMapping, clients have been able to reduce the time needed to create partnerships by 75 percent —or in real time, lowering the 18- to 24-month cycle to just 5 months. Revenue has jumped fortyfold, from $35,000 to $3 million on average. The initial partnership development discussion now can average one two-hour meeting as opposed to six separate two-hour sessions. Behind these statistics are smart partnership development practices that compress every aspect of the process. The combination of models, processes, and practices produces significant returns in an extremely short period of time.

Since the introduction of AllianceMapping in 1997, we have helped to create over 400 partnerships for service and product companies, large and small. For CEOs, serial entrepreneurs, and alliance managers, this wealth of experience translates to increased shareholder value through partnerships created at a pace never before achieved. Now presented publicly for the first time in this book, AllianceMapping can guide you to making partnerships work for your business.

Structure of the Book

I have structured the chapters based on the *order of action* a business would take when creating a partnership. Throughout the book are useful models, graphics, and tables to aid you to quickly absorb the key points. For additional reference, a glossary is included at the end of the book.

Chapter 1, "The Promise of Partnerships," presents the positive business results achieved through partnerships. When an economy is booming, partnerships are important to accelerate time to market, increase global expansion, and provide innovative products. In a neutral or downturned economy, partnerships lower the cost of goods sold, improve distribution efficiency, and decrease overhead costs. Chapter 1 identifies why companies rely on partnerships to thrive in times of economic and market change.

Chapter 2 introduces partnership types, describing the most common types of partnership structures. Examples of successful strategic and revenue-producing partnerships are introduced in case studies that will be followed throughout the book. As the firms progress from one partnership development phase to another, you will glean the processes used and the outcomes achieved, and you can often learn from their mistakes.

Chapter 3 reveals why fear and The Fatal Mistake are the greatest barriers to establishing and maintaining a profitable partnership. When considering creating a partnership relationship, anxiety, apprehension, and doubt often interfere with rational analysis. In this chapter you will learn how to identify typical concerns about partnership that different people in your organization might have—and how to get the process back on track. In this way you are able to anticipate the barrier before the partnership stalls.

Chapter 4 on AllianceMapping teaches you how to select the best partner. Through defining key attributes of your own firm and those of the potential partner, it will become clear if the target partner is truly the best choice. This simple model is absolutely vital to eliminating costly, low-return efforts while significantly increasing the results of partnerships formed.

Chapter 5 explains the steps involved in creating a viable partnership plan. After identifying the best type of partnerships for your company, you will learn how to build a partnership based on business and financial merits. As you determine the most important attributes of your company and evaluate the potential risks for your company in any partnership, you will be armed with the logic you need to construct your partnership model.

Chapter 6 details the partnership development cycle. With your plan in hand, you will learn the three phases of partnership development. This information will help you establish timelines and set expectations within your management team, ensuring that the dollars and support are in place for your partnership endeavors.

Chapter 7 describes how to effectively navigate the maze, which is the greatest mental and physical challenge to finding and talking to the right decision maker. You will become educated about the primary departments responsible for managing each potential entry point. Applying this information dramatically accelerates the rate of gaining the initial yes decision to pursue a partnership.

Chapter 8 teaches you to structure partnership agreements. Fatal mistakes are not made only during the negotiating phase. Mistakes made at that point are simply the most visible and costly mistakes. In this chapter you'll learn about the types of agreements available, and how to determine which agreement will serve your partnership the best. You will also learn how to structure your agreements to ensure the highest revenue return.

Chapter 9 identifies the tools used to create a partnership. This chapter details what is necessary for each stage of the partnership development process, including documents, as well as standard business meeting formats. Useful verbal techniques designed to ensure a response are covered so you will get maximum impact with minimal effort.

Last, Chapter 10 offers effective partnership management techniques for the long-term relationship. These strategies can also be used to accelerate the entire partnership development cycle and gain unequivocal support from your peers and management. In this chapter, you will learn from CEOs, board members, vice presidents, and other alliance managers the traits, techniques, and skills of the types of partners that they look for. Merging your background with all of this new-found know-how will ensure that you exceed the expectations of those key influencers at the potential partner and within your own company.

CHAPTER

I

The Promise
of Partnerships

CHAPTER HIGHLIGHTS

- *The partnership definition*
- *Modern partner results*
- *Alliance manager pyramid*

Under the Oak Tree

UNTIL A MERE 200 YEARS AGO, the leaders of the Basque people made partner agreements under an oak tree in Guernica. For centuries the oldest culture of Europe discussed heads-of-state agreements, treaties, and its own partnership with Spain under the old oak. As good as their word, the Basques pioneered the phrase *trust-based relationships*, forgoing written documents for oral agreements. Though the entire Basque population numbered less than a million, a governing "board" of 14 men including the leading "executive" managed the national affairs, even when dealing with the legendary King Ferdinand of Spain. Countless partnerships guaranteed trade, opened and expanded markets, and ensured Basque intellectual property and territory. The results were as impressive then as they are now. The Basques established market leadership in whaling, shipping, manufacturing, consumer foods, and even metallurgy.

Today partnerships are no less important to business innovation, growth, expansion, and market leadership. The most recent study from the consulting firm of Booz Allen Hamilton indicates that partnerships are responsible for 40 percent of revenue for companies located inside North America. A full 60 percent of revenue is attributed to alliances for firms headquartered outside North America. And the use of alliances is increasing dramatically over time. In 1980, a mere 8 percent of global companies were relying on alliances to provide revenue; 10 years later, this number had doubled to 17 percent. Recently the number of partnerships has doubled again, indicating that alliances are now used by organizations of all sizes.

In a healthy, thriving economy, partnerships are a luxury serving to accelerate revenue growth and to achieve corporate objectives such as *deeper* market penetration, *quicker* return on investment, *better* innovation, *higher* customer satisfaction, and *improved* operational efficiency or faster sales cycles. In the rolling nineties, high-growth firms in all industries created alliance departments to better serve the financial markets. This rush to the initial public offering (IPO) finish line was often accomplished by a network of companies united by a *strategic partnership*. The Wall Street favorite usually crossed the line first, thanks to the industry perception of the firm's leadership and vision as heightened through alliances.

Unfortunately, the winner too often went on to collapse because its alliances were poorly aligned. Traditional manufacturing, retail, consumer goods, health care, and even highly conservative financial services firms joined the technology crowd in placing risky partnership bets. Caught up in the hype of "the deal," short-term revenue was sacrificed for long-term strategic and sustainable partnership results.

Now we find ourselves in a swaying economy in which alliances have moved beyond luxury status to being considered an imperative for any company to survive and thrive. For the first time, the term *smart alliances* might actually be justified, as business professionals solve critical business issues by creatively applying partnerships. These smart partner strategies reduce costs and risk, enabling a company to survive in an unfavorable economic climate by eliminating the following:

- The need for new equipment and capital, a need that can be met by creating a manufacturing partnership
- The need for an expensive engineering staff, whose expertise can be accessed through an engineering partnership
- The need for costly overseas offices set up to penetrate a new market, which can be obtained as readily through a joint sales and distribution partnership
- The need for operational inefficiencies by shutting down an under-producing division and replacing it with a network of inventory, warehouse, and supply chain partnerships

Creatively employed smart partnerships are the key to thriving in any economy. Constructed well, such partnerships lead to increased—and sometimes new—business and market development. On a larger scale, partnerships help businesses achieve long-term goals such as the following:

- Establishing a new industry through joint development
- Building customer loyalty and repeat business through sales, service, and support partnerships
- Creating a template for global expansion using local and state government partnerships
- Penetrating new markets through a joint venture with a low-cost competitor
- Maintaining core competency and financial stability through partner equity investment
- Controlling costs and maintaining a loyal supplier channel through partner acquisition

Today's foremost business leaders have experienced success using these same partner strategies. In the following chapters, you will learn how small to midsize companies have harnessed the power of partnerships to create and ultimately achieve the highest value for their businesses. A preview of their results is impressive:

- A 30-person arena sports leasing company grew $500,000 to $4 million in three years relying on local government partnerships to use land at marginal cost.

- A 200-person hay and grain company grew from $15 million to $95 million over 10 years through marketing and distribution agreements.
- A 23-person boat lift manufacturer grew from $50,000 to $900,000 in 12 months through manufacturing and engineering agreements.

The Honcho's Definition of a Partnership

One of the few Basque words to become part of the English language is *honcho*. To Basques, the word described a wealthy and powerful rural landowner. Whereas the Basque honcho crafted many of the local and regional partnerships, in popular American culture, the honcho is the head of a company or the final decision maker in a given situation.

During the course of my work in partner development, I've asked a number of honchos how they defined a "partnership." While honchos used the words *alliance* and *partnership* interchangeably, they also used three other terms consistently: *bidirectional*, *core competency*, and *value driven*. The business leaders agreed that for a partnership to be considered bidirectional, each entity involved must achieve a business objective. It is not uncommon for one business to meet its objective by taking advantage of the other firm's core competency, or specialty. As this occurs, value is created for both parties in a new capacity.

Introducing the Alliance Manager

Gone are the days when every company can afford to employ a dedicated and experienced *alliance manager*—the individual responsible for creating and managing a partnership. More often than not, alliances are the responsibility of the CEO, or if the organization goes deep, a product manager. Yet the task of partner development can fall to anyone within an organization. For the purposes of simplicity, I'm going to refer to anyone primarily responsible for creating partnerships as the "alliance manager." That person might be an entrepreneur working in his or her basement or a business development manager at a multinational corporation. Yet the partner development component of the role is the same: to deliver value to the company through partnerships.

Surprisingly, these roles might have more in common than it first appears. The CEO of a one-person firm wears many hats and is ultimately responsible for the profit and loss of the business. The same is true with the group product manager at a very large corporation. Equally, neither the CEO nor the product manager has a deep or thorough understanding of the partner development process, pitfalls, and particulars.

The *alliance manager pyramid* (Figure 1–1) distinguishes between the size of the company, its available human and financial resources, and the title of the individual typically responsible for alliances.

According to the U.S. Census Bureau, over 20 million small businesses presently operate in the United States. While small businesses are expected to have fewer than 99 employees, statistics from the Small Business Administration (SBA) and *Inc.* magazine suggest the vast majority have fewer than 10 employees. In fact, the latest phrase concocted by the SBA for companies of this size is *microenterprise*. In this environment, financial and human capital require that the CEO be the innovator, entrepreneur, business manager, operations specialist, sales team, customer services support, CFO, and alliance manager.

When a firm exceeds 50 employees, it is still relatively small, and it may not be able to afford to transfer all of the alliance responsibility to another individual. In this situation, the CEO may manage the executive

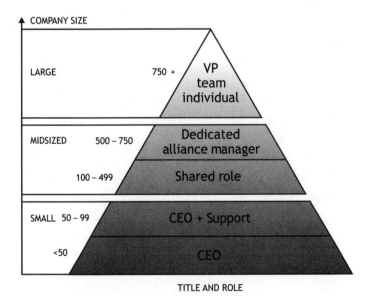

Figure 1–1   Alliance Manager Pyramid

relationship and significant milestones of the partnership, while someone else in the firm supports the day-to-day needs of the relationship.

Once a firm exceeds 100 employees, it usually assumes a textbook infrastructure. As a midsize firm, its employees may number from 100 to 750, and the alliance management tasks may be either shared or dedicated. Midsize firms may divide alliance duties between product, marketing, and even engineering managers. In any case, the CEO still has input, access, and visibility to partnerships on a regular basis.

In contrast, in a large organization with over 1000 employees, dedicated alliance managers identify, create, and manage partnerships for product lines and marketing initiatives. Corporate-wide partnerships are also handled at this level. An executive is assigned to oversee the alliance team and provide status reports to the CEO. In large organizations, the involvement of the CEO is relegated to only the most strategic decision-making activities. Initial visibility and support of a strategic partnership are followed by the official signing of the partner agreement, and later by the executive sponsor in the marketplace.

The degree of alliance success is not related to the size of a company. Rather, it results from the frequency with which dedicated alliance managers create partnerships that contribute to a successful outcome. This success then ultimately contributes significantly to the revenue derived from partnerships. Alliance managers at midsize and small companies have just as much opportunity to create successful partnerships as the big guys. A microenterprise CEO might be much more successful at developing partnerships than a large-company alliance manager if the frequency of partnership creation is consistent.

Experience in creating partnerships is not a prerequisite for success. In fact, I'd wager that the majority of partnerships are created today by first-timers. Although some of these partnerships may have taken longer than necessary to develop and may have been fraught with easily avoidable snags, nonetheless they have produced real monetary and strategic gains.

2

Types of Partnerships

CHAPTER HIGHLIGHTS

- *The basis of partnerships)*
- *Target market circle of influence*
- *Three types of product bundling*

PARTNERSHIPS CAN ACCOMPLISH great things for companies. The key to successful partnerships is creating the type that is most likely to meet the needs of the businesses involved. This chapter introduces the most prevalent types of partnerships and how they were employed to achieve tremendous results.

Sixteenth-Century Partnerships

In the thirteenth century, the Basques sought to establish themselves as an integral asset to the European continent. The first order of business was to determine what they could produce and when they needed to partner with another country. The second task was to create manufacturing and distribution relationships that secured their position as a dominant power.

By the fourteenth century, the Basques were the leading providers of iron in Europe, supplying approximately one third of the iron ore. At the same time, they sought trade agreements with producers in burgeoning territories. Having created their trading dominance with partnerships in Europe, in the sixteenth century, the Basques went on to create a number of trading agreements with Canada and the Native Americans in North America. These were some of the most important distribution agreements that had ever been created with manufacturers in the new world, particularly in America. By the seventeenth century, the Basques had pioneered distributing Native American products in Europe, from the rubber ball to tobacco. Working with only trust-based relationships, the Basques were able to partner with a host of different cultures, including French-Canadians, over a dozen Native American tribes, and European settlers first on the east coast and later in the south and southwest.

Defining a Real Partnership

A true partnership between companies exists when joint efforts are multifaceted, in that they are conducted in two or more areas of business. This characteristic differentiates a partnership from a single-facet relationship with a vendor, supplier, or service organization.

To successfully manage and support a multifaceted partnership, one or both firms must increase, extend, or create its existing business practice to support the specific needs of its new partner. Examples of this include assigning new marketing or sales personnel to the efforts of the partnership, custom training existing employees toward the partnership, adding service or support staff, changing the direction of product design and development, or making a significant monetary investment in the new endeavor.

Types of Partnerships

An easy way to classify partnerships is by the corporate objective being met. Coincidentally, this classification also identifies the functional department ultimately accountable for the success of the partnership.

Manufacturing Partnerships

Many people believe that a simple contract to deliver an order for a company is a partnership. Their understanding of a partnership could not be further from the truth. On the contrary, a manufacturing partnership needs to include an investment in personnel, equipment, processes, or other capital expenditures that a company would not otherwise allocate for its own product. This spending impacts the objectives of operations and also human resources, engineering, customer service, and finance. Additionally, a manufacturing partnership includes two partnership aspects that bind the companies in a way a customer-supplier relationship does not.

Manufacturing partnerships in particular can be used to offload a company's growing pains, which keeps its part of the business "short and profitable," according to Sunstream Corporation's CEO Ken Hey. As a designer of boat lift products, Hey placed the risk of hiring people and equipment, two undertakings that are very capital intensive, onto the infrastructure of his new partner, Elliott Bay Manufacturing. Because Hey created this manufacturing partnership at the earliest stages of his business, he was free from these burdens, as well as the need for outside financing.

Another way in which manufacturing partnerships add value is in head count. Typically, most companies that design and manufacture a product come to a crossroads where they have to determine whether the company is a research organization or a manufacturer. When a company divorces itself from the manufacturing process through a partnership, two things often occur. First, because the engineers are not tied to the manufacturing process, they are free to create new products or improve existing ones to retain customers. As Hey found, "With the increased focus on the customer, we build a wide breadth of product line, where we can create a variety of products for their needs."

A manufacturing partnership can also enhance a company's competitive position in pricing its products. Production cost savings resulting from the partnership can result in a dramatically lower cost to the consumer. In Hey's case, his partner, Elliott Bay Manufacturing, employs a portion of the state's prison workforce. Once released, many of these former prisoners become employees. The specialized workforce is trained by Elliott Bay to a high quality standard, but it is not as expensive as more traditional machine shop workers.

Mitch Mounger, CEO of branding and promotions firm Sunrise Identity, uses manufacturing partnerships to ensure that his largest customers don't bypass his company when purchasing apparel. Mounger knew that several of his clients, including Starbucks, Microsoft, and

Haines, were outsourcing some of their apparel orders overseas cheaper, even though they were using the same supplier. As Mounger looked for ways to stop the bleeding, he realized that if he expanded his product offerings, such as incorporating screen printing on T-shirts, he would be justified in purchasing large quantities of apparel. Consequently, he created a direct partnership with an overseas manufacturer, thereby lowering his costs, which enabled him to beat the prices his competitors were charging. In addition, he was also able to add customization either at the overseas factory or on his own premises.

For manufacturing partnerships to work, the partnership needs to be exclusive to one or both parties, thereby preventing either from working with a competitor. For instance, Sunstream and Elliott Bay both severed ties with organizations thought to be competitive to the other firm. This loss of available vendors motivates both entities to ensure that their partnership is profitable, and in turn signals the importance of the relationship to both teams. Successful manufacturing partnerships also allow one or both partners the *right of first refusal*, which means that a company can prevent its manufacturing partner from taking on potentially competitive business. This ensures complete disclosure and a more open communication environment.

Engineering Partnerships

An engineering partnership is not dissimilar from a manufacturing partnership. In fact, the intent and objective of the relationships are nearly identical. The primary difference is that the up-front costs incurred by the engineering firm are offset in some way by a share of revenue or ownership of intellectual property. This extends a simple service provider contract to a risk- and profit-sharing partnership.

Engineering partnerships are created to combat a talent and financial scarcity. Sunstream again partnered with then-third-year engineering student Matthew Freeborn's company, Idea Design and Development, for extra engineering help. According to Hey, the engineering partnership was and still is advantageous to both firms. "We helped him get his business off the ground, and he aided us in manufacturing specific aspects of our product that could not be produced by Elliott Bay," explained Hey. Sunstream wasn't paying cash for the engineering time, saving significantly on the research and development costs. However, when orders came in, Sunstream did pay for the manufacturing. Idea

Design and Development was hungry to develop a brand, customer list, and its own style. This engineering partnership was creatively employed to get both businesses off the ground, and it used the right motivations to ensure continued output.

Another way an engineering firm elects to reduce its risk in the partnership is by taking an ownership stake in the intellectual property created during the partnership. The royalty payout streams might even last for a period of years after the partnership ceases to exist. A California-based consumer foods company employed this term when creating a new cookie for a large foods conglomerate. In exchange for promotion and guaranteed royalties, the intellectual property associated with the cookie would be turned over after a period of years.

Field Sales Partnerships

Even if you have your own sales force or distribution channels, partnerships designed to aid field sales activity can be very important. This type of partnership shortens the sales cycle and can improve the customer experience. The combination of the two benefits helps retain existing customers and attract new customers, and it can erect competitive barriers.

Six-year-old Bite Footwear, one of the fastest-growing sport shoe companies in America, literally doubled its sales when it created two field sales partnerships. CEO Dale Bathum's firm tried to hire independent sales representatives in Canada and on the east coast, but they quickly found that the quality of service, support, and even knowledge of these representatives was poor. Furthermore, as a specialty golf shoe manufacturer, the independent sales representatives were not able to leverage long-term customer relationships common in the golfing industry.

Based on this costly experience, Bathum redesigned field sales partnerships with new golfing industry sales firms located in each territory. Each firm has an established clientele and is seeking to augment its product offering list. The bottom-line impact to Bite Footwear has been "a doubling of our business," recounts Bathum. In addition to the sales, the margins are much higher than a normal field partnership since Bathum's partners manage the front- and back-end service aspects. "If an account wants the shoes, it calls into their customer service departments," said Bathum. This requires the field sales partner to shoulder the infrastructure costs while giving Bathum's firm higher margins.

Addressing customer support not only improves margins, it has a direct impact on shareholder return. Billion-dollar Network Appliance develops storage solutions for large customers who often spend hundreds of thousands of dollars on a single order. According to CEO Dan Wormenhoven, "The customer expectation is close to perfect" for every interaction with Network Appliance, from the first sales call to the delivery, implementation, and service. In an environment where you can only go down in the eyes of the customer, your field partners are vital to ensuring that the customer is satisfied.

Network Appliance field partners IBM and Accenture have not only helped to significantly improve annual revenue greatly; they have ensured Network Appliance's corporate survival. Through partnering with these corporate giants, Network Appliance has been invited into a variety of new deals it otherwise had neither the visibility nor the access to participate in.

Customer Retention through Field Agreements Furniture and office equipment dealers seem to be on every street corner. The barriers to entry are low, competition is high, and margins are usually thin. Sean O'Brien invested in Business Interiors Northwest, which at the time was a 13-year-old company with revenues of $17 million. Today, Business Interiors Northwest has three locations, 135 employees, and revenues approaching $50 million. At the time, customer retention was less complex and more transactional in nature. Today, customer retention requires multidimentional relationships and national service capabilities that integrate technology throughout the process.

An exiting relationship with global office furniture manufacturer, Herman Miller, Inc., presented a unique opportunity for O'Brien to influence a national service strategy aimed at retaining large corporate customers with multiple locations. A Herman Miller dealer network steering council was formed with the top 15 dealers across the country. The result was a Herman Miller Certified Network of 50 dealers connected via the Web who are committed to providing consistent, best-in-class service to national customers. In O'Brien's words, "We now have true capabilities in retaining our national customers for life."

Field Sales with Government Agencies By the time Michael Nelson purchased filing system dealer Tab Northwest in 1996, it had established itself as a leading provider of high-density storage and filing systems and supplies, yet it was hemorrhaging money badly. Nelson was determined to make the company profitable through several smart partnerships with government agencies.

Nelson knew a number of his existing customers were local, state, and district government offices or affiliates. What he found was most of them were motivated to purchase from state-employed sales representatives who take the office supply orders of governmental agencies. When he learned this, Nelson's new business goal was to become the state's joint field sales partner for his specialized storage and filing systems.

Nelson provided a value proposition wherein the sales representative would identify the opportunity for Tab's mobile systems. Once done, Tab Northwest would measure, prepare the cost estimate, order, install, service, and support the product line.

Within weeks, Tab Northwest's own eight sales representatives were augmented by another dozen state sales representatives. After a year of calling on the state agency, Tab enjoyed near exclusive contracts with many of the state's largest accounts. Revenues have since doubled from $2.5 million to over $5 million in less than two years. Direct contracts with many agencies are now in place, and the partnership template is being extended to other states with the same operational system. At all times, Nelson has kept his risk low. "We broadened out sales opportunities in a way that didn't require me to pay for additional sales personnel until products were sold," he confided.

This field partnership requires ongoing training of state sales representatives and marketing support from both companies. This monetary and time commitment differentiates it from a standard sales contract, wherein a representative would receive a commission for an extended sale. The front-to-finish sales cycle draws these companies into a close partnership. Both have invested in the effort and are mutually rewarded with repeat customer business.

Operations Partnerships

In supporting the corporate goals of a company, operations departments often create partnerships to lower the costs of goods sold. This in turn reduces the time to getting the company off the ground, as well as the time getting the product to market. More importantly, such partnerships reduce the need for lengthy, expensive property leases that can be risky during market downturns, and they can offer flexibility in moving into new geographic territories quickly.

Two examples of such relationships are facilities partnerships and land partnerships. In achieving the corporate objectives of cost reduction and operational efficiency, facilities and land partnerships are pivotal. These are two of the least sexy types of partnerships, and as a consequence, they are the least understood and the most underused. But there is no denying that facilities and land partnerships save cold hard cash.

Facilities Partnerships Facilities partnerships are those in which one firm utilizes a portion of its partner's building in return for a fee. As opposed to a simple rent arrangement wherein a set rent is paid every month, a facilities partnership is based on customized terms, shared risk, and unlimited financial rewards. It also provides no guarantees for either party and has a particularly high risk for the builder-owner.

Smart facilities partnerships take advantage of the willingness of each entity to share the risk and reward associated with a growing business. Consider, for example, the company Espresso Connection. Profiled as one of the fastest-growing companies in the country by *Inc.* magazine, when Espresso Connection was first formed in 1996, it lacked the funds to purchase real estate or enter into costly leases for its coffee stands. Furthermore, due to wild cash flow fluctuations associated with the unpredictable revenues at start-up locations, the company could not sign the long-term leases demanded by building owners.

CEO Christian Karr realized that the only way to get his company off the ground was to find a landlord or building owner who would extend Karr the space long enough for him to determine if his business model would work. Doing so was risking space allocation without payment, as occupation by Espresso Connection meant that another tenant could not rent the space.

Implementing this strategy would require that a potential partner have a certain personality. Specifically, Karr was looking for a landlord or building owner with a tendency to look for profit from speculative investments. The potential partner would also have to have a fair amount of small spaces that were either unsuitable for a larger tenant or overly costly to build out. Karr found what he was looking for in a mall owner.

The facilities agreement Karr ultimately constructed was a partnership wherein the building owner supplied the space at no charge, instead receiving a monthly payment based on current revenues. The downside of this arrangement was zero rent in the short term, but the upside was the potential to realize an enormous profit, much more than the rent would have amounted to over the long term.

This partnership turned out to be a tremendous windfall for the owner who took a chance on Espresso Connection. As Karr did not place a rent cap in the original space agreements, the rent his company paid out was over three times what the space would have yielded had the building owner signed Espresso Connection to a standard contract and up to 10 times in certain locations. In fact, the first stands grossed over a quarter of a million dollars annually. The building owner also benefited from the partnership as Karr included an option to renew the contract under the same terms.

The original facilities partnership model has been used over several hundred times as Espresso Connection has expanded its locations. The terms have changed slightly in favor of Espresso Connection, which now places limits on the percentage of revenue. Inversely balancing the percentage of revenue with the time in the location has delivered a more reasonable payout schedule to the building owners while improving Espresso Connection's margins. According to Karr, it has also allowed him to get into markets "at least a year faster than competitors searching to find space, customize an existing space, and then open the door for business."

Land Partnerships   A land partnership is often combined with a facilities partnership to further collapse product time to market. Arena Sports, another adrenaline-inducing company, was brought to life using both facilities and land partnerships, which literally took two years off the timeline associated with a traditional land purchase.

CEO Don Crowe, a former chief financial officer and lifelong soccer enthusiast, decided to bring soccer to the masses through indoor sports arenas. The biggest challenges he faced were first, to obtain reasonably priced land in the middle of an economic upswing, in which land prices were climbing, and second, financing the enormous building costs associated with creating an indoor arena.

After crunching the numbers, he realized his business model would not be feasible without utilizing partnerships. A quick glance in his own hometown identified the largest owner of unusable land to be the local city and state governments. Crowe learned that state and local governments have lots of real estate and no money to do anything with it, as they are often restricted by land use ordinances as well as the high cost of developing community-oriented buildings.

Crowe's value proposition to the city was a partnership wherein the government would develop the arena and retain ownership of the building and the land. The lease was structured in such a way that the cost of the building construction would be subsidized through the lease with Arena Sports, who would be responsible for the mortgage. This eliminated the need for the government to raise taxes or even to bring the transaction in front of the voters. It also placed the management in the hands of a professional organization determined to be profitable, rather than a not-for-profit government entity.

This initial partnership model was replicable as well. Just as Karr reused the facility partnership model, so too did Crowe, leveraging his land and facility partnership model in multiple cities and regions. In fact, he designed this model to cross national borders. He has already extended into Europe and South America, and he has no plans to stop. Revenues of Arena Sports have grown from $0.5 million in 1999 to over $4 million in 2002. With less than 10 employees, this growth is directly attributable to operations partnerships.

Distribution Partnerships

In a distribution partnership, one organization allows the partner to distribute and sell its product. Because the primary goal is to create revenue, the sales organization is usually responsible for the distribution partnerships. While this gives an immediate uplift to revenues, it accomplishes the more strategic goals of penetrating new markets and raising the barriers to competition. It also has the power to create partners out of customers, turning a single company into a foothold for an entire market. This is known as a *market aggregator*, perhaps the most strategic result of a distribution partnership possible.

Distribution agreements range from the simple to the complex. In a simple distribution relationship, coffee table board game manufacturer

Front Porch Classics partnered with Barnes & Noble Booksellers to distribute a new a board game it created for the college crowd. In this partnership, Front Porch's *Cram!* board game is sold at every Barnes & Noble that is located near or on a U.S. college campus.

What differentiates this distribution partnership from a standard retail sales contract is the degree to which Front Porch solicited and received input while creating the board game. Front Porch was looking to match Barnes & Noble's thinking toward a specific market. Cofounder Steve Edmiston knew that the only way to do this was to create a board game addressing the qualities of a particular consumer— namely, lifestyle-driven college students frequenting higher-end coffee shops and bookstores.

Front Porch Classics sought and received input on the board game from targeted retailers, including Barnes & Noble. This alignment caused both to continue seeking a product that would "provoke a feeling and an experience" for their target customer.

As a result, Front Porch Classics "sent them the final prototype on a Friday and on Monday received a purchase order," explained Edmiston. This distribution partnership allows for design and development participation for future target markets. It also includes marketing assistance, product review, and support for Front Porch Classics.

The Leveraged Approach   Anderson Hay and Grain, a producer of feed for race horses and other livestock with particular dietary needs, provides us with another example of a simple distribution agreement. Before creating a distribution partnership with a Pacific Rim–based firm, only a few distribution channels were open to Anderson in Japan. Once the agreement was final to make its single distribution partner a marketing arm with input into future business strategy, Anderson found that its Asian partner opened an additional 30 distribution channels within Japan. This immediately tripled the business within that particular territory. It also had the effect of raising the barrier significantly to Anderson's competitors.

Anderson started with distribution agreements designed to increase revenue, penetrate a new market, and gain a competitive advantage. By motivating his partner, each was able to use the distributor as an aggregator, gaining exposure and sales into a new market segment without any additional work.

Complex Distribution Partnerships   An example of a complex distribution agreement is one wherein a company decides to expand its strategic offerings by selling additional products or services related to its core business. For example, a Washington, D.C.–based software services organization desired to build its revenue and margins. One way it could achieve this corporate objective was to modify its distribution agreement with software provider Comdisco Systems to include product licensing. The strategy it employed included licensing Comdisco Systems generic software, which it then customized to fit a particular market application. Additional fees would be generated on engineering development required by customer customization at the beginning of the contract, and the associated fees paid for the software customer support and maintenance.

To make this strategy successful, the firm had to offer engineering, customer support, and maintenance consulting services. The price it was able to charge far exceeded the one-time cost of building the organization. At the same time, this strategy effectively blocked potential competitors from providing ongoing consulting fees.

In return for this commitment to its product line, Comdisco provided local and regional marketing, technical, and sales support to the firm. Additionally, the firm became the beneficiary of nationwide sales referrals from the Comdisco sales team, who quickly learned about the customized application it had developed using Comdisco's technology. It was neither geographic nor industry specific and was therefore useful around the country. This was a strategic market advantage to the company at a critical time in its growth. Revenue from this single partnership delivered more than 40 percent of the firm's revenue within the ensuing 18 months.

Hard, Soft, and Marketing Bundling   Depending on the buying and product-use habits of joint customers, partners may elect to combine products before presenting the final package to the market. The way in which the final package is delivered is known as *bundling*. Licensing and distribution partnerships detail the manner in which products are to be bundled for a particular market.

The three most common bundling options for delivering product solutions to customers are hard, soft, and market bundling:

- *Hard bundling:* Two solutions are physically integrated or combined at the time of manufacture.
- *Soft bundling:* Two solutions are packaged together, but they are not physically integrated.
- *Market bundling:* Two solutions are marketed together, but they are not packaged together.

A simple distribution agreement commonly incorporates soft bundling. Neither product requires changes. Two products are packaged, promoted, and delivered to a particular audience. In either model, the marketing is conducted either jointly or separately while the financial, support, and service aspects of the bundle are managed separately by both firms. It is a very clean transaction and supports broader partnership objectives.

A hard bundle is used when the customer either can't or won't spend the time to integrate two products after purchase. This necessitates that the partners integrate the products at the time of manufacturing. In this model, the revenue is invoiced and received by the entity shipping the product. Service, support, and marketing are almost always the responsibility of the shipping partner as well. This is because the product being bundled within the primary solution is usually, but not always, visible. The Intel microprocessor, for example, is hard bundled into the Dell, Hewlett-Packard, and other types of computers. Revenue is provided from the computer manufacturer to Intel.

On the other hand, the free AOL CD I received with my last video purchase is an example of a soft bundle. The two products are packaged separately but held together with cellophane shrink-wrap. If I elect to sign up with AOL, I send my payments directly to AOL. A marketing bundle would have existed if the AOL CD had been uniquely customized for a particular video rental chain and was a part of an integrated marketing campaign with joint logos and offers printed on the packaging of each firm.

Product Integration Partnerships

When the primary intent of a solution is to ensure product interoperability, the partnership is created and managed out of a product group. Products are integrated to ensure that a solution functions, but this type of agreement does not require the products to be bundled in any fashion. It simply means product integration work has been completed by the manufacturers of the products, and a customer purchasing both products can be assured each functions properly with the other.

Joint Development Partnerships

A joint development agreement is created to continue, accelerate, or improve a product innovation. This arrangement can be used to innovate or improve existing products, or it can be used to create entirely new applications for a product. When Sunstream Corporation was looking to improve its product line, it created a joint development partnership with Cobalt Corporation after several years of working together in the field. Under the joint development agreement, Sunstream will take its knowledge of boat lifts and tailor it to a new line of Cobalt personal watercrafts. While the engineering team will contribute the most heavily to the partnership during its initial phases, each department at both organizations will ultimately be involved in making the new product line a success. Product marketing and manufacturing will ensure product delivery, and marketing will handle promotion and sales, service, and support the customer interaction. This partnership was a true combination of best-of-breed knowledge and products into a solution which makes sense for the personal watercraft owner.

On a different scale, a joint development partnership was created by 15-person company The Finest Accessories and electronics giant Motorola. Motorola's cellular phone accessory division asked CEO Laurie Erickson of France Luxe hair clips to create cellular phone faceplates.

After three months of working together on prototypes, Motorola approved the first batch of faceplates. The entire design, development, and manufacturing process was controlled by The Finest Accessories, who was able to retain ownership of the resulting technology, designs, and other intellectual property. Yet her team works with over 20 Motorola divisions, including product, consumer, marketing, and operations, during every aspect of production, from design to development. As a small company of less than $3 million, the initial investment of about $30,000 in travel expenses paid off in the first two orders. The bidirectional exclusive relationship is expected to triple Erickson's business within 12 months.

Original Equipment Manufacturing Partnership

A partnership through which one company provides its product to another, which is then self-branded, is known as an *original equipment manufacturing* (OEM) *partnership*. In this scenario, one company submerges its own brand to its partner in return for a higher fee. Reducing costs is a tremendous motivator for using an OEM partnership, as is getting a product to market faster, and effectively reducing a competitive threat.

For instance, medical equipment manufacturer Instromedix, a mid-sized $100 million firm, created a noninvasive pacemaker monitor. At the time, the firm consisted of approximately 125 people, while its competitor was 30,000 strong.

Instromedix showed early prototypes to the competitor in hopes of a joint development partnership but was initially rebuffed. It wasn't until Instromedix brought its final product to market and demonstrated its superiority that its competitor sought to attain the technology. The two companies clashed, as privately held Instromedix did not desire to be acquired, while the competitor would sell only those products carrying its name.

The result was the creation of a joint development partnership wherein both firms would work together on future products. However, the advantage for the competitor was the creation of an immediate OEM agreement. Under the agreement, the pacemaker monitor device is created by Instromedix but it is packaged under the name of its competitor. Instromedix is completely transparent to the buyer or user of the device.

Espresso Connection also deftly turned a competitor into a partner by "OEMing" the coffee beans of Java Trading Company. When it was just a coffee stand owner, Espresso Connection decided it could make more money faster by diversifying into the bean roasting business. As the highest margin side of a coffee retail business, Espresso Connection switched suppliers to OEM the beans from Java Trading Company. In the process, Karr saved more than a dollar per pound and was able to place the Espresso Connection brand name on the coffee bag. Prior to that time, Karr was buying from Seattle's Best Coffee, which was charging more for the coffee and requiring brand recognition.

OEM as the Company Cornerstone   Another company using OEM partnerships is Actify, a software company launched in the winter of 2002. Instead of incorporating OEM partnership as one prong on its partnership model, Actify is utilizing the OEM philosophy as the cornerstone of growth for the small company. OEM partnerships both establish market dominance in North America while allowing resellers in the Pacific Rim to provide customer value through integration and consulting services. Said CEO Mike Walsh, "Without OEM partnerships at this stage we are dead."

Actify has developed what it calls the "Adobe PDF for computer-aided design (CAD) applications." Actify's software allows large designs (2 feet by 2 feet and beyond) to be electronically captured and shared. Today companies such as General Motors, Boeing, and other manufacturers use expensive and sophisticated design systems, but they cannot easily share designs electronically. Furthermore, design departments within different divisions and locations often select and use their own CAD software, making interoperability impossible. Not only is this an operational nightmare but it is also a financial fiasco: The costs of having different and often incompatible software residing on each computer desktop reaches into the hundreds of thousands of dollars. To make matters worse, outside the organization, vendors within the supply chain are using different CAD software, nearly ensuring conflict.

By comparison, Actify's software solution costs merely $1000 per user, which is a comparative bargain. It eliminates the need to print out cumbersome documents or visit the site that has produced the drawings, whether this is across the country or world.

"If we signed a major deal with a product lifecycle management (PLM) solutions provider, and they embed our solution," said Walsh, "they have included our unique features that are absolutely needed in the marketplace." The PLM provider increases the market's perception of the company as an innovative company striving to improve the customer experience. At the same time, it creates demand in the marketplace for features available only from Actify.

This initial activity looks like a simple technology sale on the surface, but embedding agreements are much more than a simple sale. Folding one product into another is a complex and time-consuming process involving joint product planning to align short- and long-term customer solutions. It then requires the product development and engineering expertise to understand the particulars of merging two different product sets. Marketing must be involved to solve the questions about product positioning as well as customer, vendor, or supplier messages. The sales force must be informed of, and if possible trained in, the differentiators and benefits of the product integration. Finally, finance and operations must understand how to track and account for the revenue associated with the embedded agreement.

It is for these reasons that many relationships starting with an embedding agreement grow in complexity and can contribute significantly to the bottom line and continue over a long period of time. The very nature of an embedding agreement requires a deep understanding of the partners' business. New opportunities, ideas, and products are a natural outcome of cross-divisional working relationships.

By using embedding agreements, Actify is wisely setting the stage for immediate market penetration with an eye toward long-term sustainable growth. The up-front cost requirements necessary to create an embedding agreement are infinitesimal compared to the return on investment.

If pacemaker monitoring and design-sharing CAD software are hard to grasp, you need look no further than your local clothing store to identify an OEM partnership. Every-day examples include hair products, shoes, or other retail items purchased by a large company and sold under its own name. For example, retail chain Nordstrom carries name-brand shoes along with "house-brand" shoes carrying the Nordstrom name. In a number of cases, the products are made by the same manufacturer. Yet the cost to the consumer is significantly lower for the Nordstrom shoe because one entity is being removed in the retail distribution chain.

Marketing Partnerships

Marketing partnerships are critical to many businesses trying to create product awareness and demand. They are also a way to save cash by dovetailing a new product with an older product that has a known image and/or brand name. For those firms such as software manufacturers who rely almost entirely on third parties to build market share for additional products, marketing partnerships are vital.

Espresso Connection has saved millions of dollars through marketing partnerships. As the CEO of a fledgling company, Karr created a marketing and OEM partnership with Seattle's Best Coffee. In return for using its beans, Espresso Connection has launched its own image as a "mobile provider" of Seattle's Best Coffee. In this way, Espresso Connection's logo and tagline has been promoted on billboards, brochures, ads, and in a great many other marketing campaigns all paid for and produced by its partner.

Even billion-dollar Microsoft needs marketing partnerships. Steve Murchie, a product manager for the SQL Server Group at Microsoft, notes that fewer than 50 percent of customers create their own internal software applications using SQL Server. The remainder use Microsoft partners to assist the customer community in using SQL Server. Marketing is vital to help the partners get to market.

One marketing relationship that stands out to Murchie is Microsoft's partnership with Pro Clarity. When it was just a seven-person firm, this business intelligence software provider from Boise, Idaho, approached Murchie and announced that its product directly competed with SQL Server. However, Pro Clarity also said that it would be open to complementing SQL Server, and it provided a few ideas on how it could improve SQL Server's technology.

This in-your-face approach paid off when Pro Clarity found a way to leverage the SQL Server core technology and combine it with its own to create a market differentiator in the business intelligence space. When the Pro Clarity team had incorporated SQL Server technology and completed its initial product, the team came back with a finished product. It so impressed Murchie and the Microsoft SQL Server group that Pro Clarity was asked to demonstrate the product in a keynote presentation at an upcoming conference.

This placed the small business at center stage in front of hundreds of Microsoft sales and marketing managers. Based on this response, Microsoft placed a demo version of *Pro Clarity* on Microsoft's promotional CD that the company sent to tens of thousands of employees and partners, including the entire worldwide technical and sales staff. The time frame from the first conversation to the first keynote address at a sales conference was a short two and a half months. It took an additional three to six months for the field sales representatives to adopt and start pushing the Pro Clarity product.

In this case, the marketing partnership was significant for both firms. The formal relationship enabled Microsoft to show the rest of the company, and the entire computer industry, a new application requiring SQL Server. This had the effect of generating a number of incremental sales for Murchie's product line. The relationship in turn enabled Pro Clarity to get its company off the ground in a rocket-booster-like fashion, riding on the coattails of Microsoft's marketing machine.

Partnerships Formed Because of Philosophical Alignment

Aside from the various strategic reasons partnerships are created, they are often developed on the basis of similar cultures and philosophies. Two firms engaged in a retail distribution arrangement do not need to share either cultural or philosophical similarities in order to succeed in a joint business endeavor. A partnership, on the other hand, will succeed more readily if the value traits, goals, and vision are as well aligned as the core competency of the product lines.

CEOs mention two words more than any others when determining if a partnership is going to succeed: *philosophy* and *culture*. Congruence in both areas influences not only the tenor of the partnership but also the requirement of a formal partnership. It also impacts the terms within the partnership agreement.

Kathryn Karver of Focused Training chose Shandel Slaten's True Life Coaching as her service partner after assessing that the philosophies of the two companies truly matched. Like Slaten, Karver believes life coaching requires personal responsibility, responsiveness, and action. They also agree on the philosopy that coaching without tangible results is just "a bunch of psychobabble." Their mutual belief in less talk and more action set the stage for their marketing and sales agreement, which includes a calendar of marketing events, seminars, and revenue sharing.

Culture is the second cornerstone for assessing whether a partnership will work. Sometimes a cultural fit is obvious, while other times it is not. A former manager at Hewlett-Packard told me that HP used McKinsey Consulting to determine why its own partnership with Microsoft wasn't working as planned. Ultimately the report determined that the two firms "were culturally mismatched." Unfortunately, this wasn't a surprise to HP or Microsoft, but it was a very expensive validation exercise.

Sometimes two entities can have a tremendous cultural fit even though their cultures seem vastly different. Dale Bathum, CEO of Bite Footwear, has described two of his partnerships that are philosophically aligned but not outwardly visible cultural fits. Yet each is very successful. As a small manufacturer of high-end golf shoes, Bathum started his company in 1996 with an idea for a golf shoe that was closer in style to a flip-flop sandal than it was to the more traditional leather and lace shoe. Bathum approached the same manufacturers that his former employer, Nike, used in China. It took just two meetings for Bathum to create a manufacturing partnership with the company. Bathum committed to using the firm for all Bite Footwear shoe manufacturing even though he had nothing more than a prototype at the time. In return, he expected the manufacturer to extend sufficient credit, operations, and inventory services to his firm just as they did for billion-dollar Nike. This required the manufacturing firm to front both the capital investment and to carry the majority of the risk.

Within 12 months, the first shoe came off the factory floor and the year ended with sales of $200,000. The 2001 fiscal year ended with sales of over $7 million. At no point has a formal agreement ever been put in place between the two firms.

Bathum believes the philosophy of long-term relationships and quality products has been essential in creating and maintaining this crucial first partnership. A culture of trust, understanding, and respect has grounded the partnership in an environment of open communication. "It all boils down to an understanding that our manufacturing partner supports us in any reasonable way. And in return, we won't go to any other factory. It's that simple."

Compare this overseas partnership with a more unlikely partnership in the United States. Bite Footwear also partners with rocker Alice Cooper every year to host a celebrity golf tournament. The image of blood dripping from Alice Cooper's mouth on stage is quite different from the culture and philosophy embodied by environmentally friendly Bite Footwear. Yet it is Alice Cooper's Children's Foundation that matches Bite Footwear's own civic- and community-minded philosophy perfectly. Each has a desire to aid underprivileged, at-risk children. Together, they have partnered to create a celebrity golf tournament to raise money for Alice Cooper's Children's Foundation, in Phoenix, Arizona, the hometown of Bite Footwear.

After launching the first tournament in 1996, the foundation realized it needed sponsors to help support the event. At the same time, Bite Footwear was a fledgling company desperately seeking exposure to both opinion leaders and fashion trendsetters. During an initial discussion, Alice Cooper and Dale Bathum realized that both the philosophy and culture of the two organizations were perfectly aligned despite outward appearances. Using a marketing and sales outline instead of a formal agreement, the two organizations united to raise money for children's programs. Six years later, the tournament is a marquee event, luring celebrities such as Chris O'Donnell, Jerry Rice, and the band Creed to raise money for the foundation's goals. In the process, the event has made Bite Footwear believers out of some of the most hardcore golf enthusiasts in the country.

Where to Find a Partner? Target Market Circle of Influence

The majority of the 20 million small businesses out there today would be thrilled to work with a company who would help close business deals, particularly if it were at no additional cost to them. The rest of the time, the CEOs are "going to look for a shortcut" to identifying the right partner, just as Ken Hey and Christian Karr did when they needed to build their businesses.

The shortcut to identifying the right partner was born of common sense and then validated by customer feedback. Hey, Karr, and many other CEOs knew what their company needed to grow, so they sought partners by reviewing other entities serving a mutual customer or both companies in the target market. I refer to this common-sense partner identification method as the *target market circle of influence*. (Figure 2–1).

By identifying where your target market shops, plays, and works, you can easily identify potential partners. CEO Mitch Mounger is a great example of an individual who discovered that many of his company's clients, such as Starbucks, Microsoft, and Haines, were also being serviced by a firm known as Sunrise Identity. At the time, Mounger's company, LCM, was a $3 million firm, providing custom logo embroidery and design work. Clients were also using $10 million Sunrise Identity for promotional, branding, and marketing services.

A sales field integration partnership was established to prevent the two firms from competing while leveraging the nonmutual customer base to the benefit of both. Yet this was not a one-dimensional joint sales effort but instead included joint marketing and even custom product development when required by a customer. Ensuring customer satisfaction required the agreement to parse who "owned" the customer,

Figure 2–1 Target Market Circle of Influence

who would manage the daily account activities, and finally, who would oversee the accounting.

This collaboration was so successful that after a period of just three months the companies started discussing the benefits of a merger. Nine months later, a buyout was completed by Mounger's firm, which elected to keep the name Sunrise Identity. While the combined business increased, reaching $24 million in 2002, the most important result is the newly formed company's strategic positioning for future growth. "We now have the product lines, skill sets, and infrastructure to double within another two years," said Mounger.

The Best Partnership for You

Partnerships provide an opportunity to conduct business more productively, efficiently, and profitably. As you become more familiar with the concept of partnership and understand how to use it to accomplish your specific corporate objectives, you will be able to pinpoint not just the type of partnership you need but also the specific attributes the partnership should have. In so doing, you will be able to accurately discern partner development reality from myth.

CHAPTER

3

Overcoming the Fear
of Partnerships

CHAPTER HIGHLIGHTS

- *The partner development life cycle*
- *Role-based fears and the impact on the partnership*
- *The myth of The Fatal Mistake*

Using Fear as a Favorite Weapon

FRANCISCO FRANCO WAS A SMALL, squeaky-voiced, insecure man of forty who possessed an uncanny ability to inspire and lead his troops. According to writer Mark Hurlansky, Franco was one of 21 major generals in the service of the Spanish military during World War II. To the amazement of his contemporaries and historical scholars alike, Franco was able to successfully avoid scandal as he switched sides from the Spanish to the Basques, then to the Germans, and ultimately to the Americans. Each transition he effected with ease, generating a variety of partnership agreements for commerce, peace, and war with his partner *du jour.* In his 1999 book *The Basque History of the World* (Walker & Co.), Hurlansky wrote that Franco's success was attributable to his "almost naïve belief in his ability to prevail."

This ability to gain advantage over others is also credited to a talent for using "fear as his weapon," wrote Hurlansky. Using fear in combination with ruthless techniques on the battlefield and back rooms crafting strategy, the perception of Franco ultimately became a greater deterrent to his enemies than what Franco might have actually done.

Franco played up the fear factor to instill paranoia, trepidation, and suspicion on top of misconceptions, anxiety, and doubt. This spread among potential partners and enemies alike during his expansion activities. In many ways this is the same strategy large companies use to intimidate smaller potential partners into signing agreements that are advantageous to the larger company. Without the confidence that the game is being played on a level field, employees within the smaller organization lack the incentive or enthusiasm to garner support and assistance from their internal team members.

Today's dominant businesses use the fear factor mostly during negotiation. Yet most novice alliance managers believe the strategy applies throughout the entire partner development cycle. This hinders the positive, constructive tone that should be the theme of the partnership effort. Using the words James Fullbright delivered to the Senate in March 1964, these individuals are "handicapped [in their efforts] based on old myths rather than current realities."

The Partner Development Cycle

Octavio Paz believed that "contemporary man has rationalized the myths, but he has not been able to destroy them." Nor have modern-day partner development alliance managers been able to entirely remove the fear or uncertainty that partnership can evoke in organizations. Any one of these fears can be fatal to the successful creation of a partnership.

To ensure that you are not hindered by fear-created roadblocks, you need to understand the fears that correspond to the partner development cycle. Once you can predict when and from whom an apprehension will arise, you can anticipate and address the concern proactively. Doing so will generate support for the potential partnership and keep your partner development timeline on track.

Creating a partnership is a five-step process (Figure 3–1). The cycle begins with identifying and validating the best potential partner organization (PPO) through AllianceMapping and progresses to product vali-

Figure 3–1   The Partner Development Cycle

dation through a due-diligence process which results in the formation of an agreement. When this has concluded, the partnership transitions to the individual responsible for the daily maintenance of the partnership.

This road map is not unique to a particular industry or product line. Rather, it is consistent across industry, product, and alliance type. From boat manufacturing to software to consumer foods, the partner development life cycle is the first constant you may rely on.

Jim Hudson, cofounder and vice president of business development for fraud detection software firm Amcrin Corporation, also found his partner development efforts followed a prescriptive course. "We identified those who could supply us with a network infrastructure at no charge to us, we narrowed the field, and then we contacted and created a joint development agreement with Qsent. In parallel, we identified those organizations with information necessary to our service model, applied the same process and created a joint engineering agreement with Loss Control Solutions." Because Loss Control is part of an industry highly regulated but divided due to the nature of its core business (organizations reporting fraud), Hudson needed a partnership with an organization who worked with everyone. "Our third partnership was created with the Communications Fraud Control Association (CFCA), and it was accomplished using the same process of identification, validation, and creation." Most impressively, Hudson is a former police officer who had never run a company before or created a single alliance in his life. He just applied common sense to his strategy, and it paid off handsomely.

Shandel Slaten, CEO of True Life Coaching, found this process to be valid when creating two partnerships for her sole-proprietorship consulting practice. She created joint marketing and sales partnerships with Focused Training and Axxis Consulting after isolating potential targets, validating a need, and establishing the partnership. She transitioned into the management of the partnership with ease: "I'd done my homework on the front end" by aligning the companies properly.

During the course of your career, you might jump from industry to industry. Or you might stay at one large company but work on many different product lines. Whatever the case, you need consistent methodologies so that your partner development techniques can mature. As this happens, your portfolio of tools such as presentations, value propositions, and final agreements will become a golden repository.

When you master the details of a partner development process, you become empowered with three vital attributes associated with long-term sustainable partnership results: *consistency*, *replicability*, and *leveragability*. A *consistent* process enables you to *replicate*, or duplicate, your efforts without significant change or modification. This means your efforts are highly *leveraged*, or more effective, efficient, and monetarily rewarding. It also means your efforts can be extended from one partner organization to another. This has the effect of multiplying the return on your efforts. If you are working within a team environment, this return is exponential as your processes and tools are used time and again with minimal change. The immediate result is better-quality output in less time with dramatically better results.

Fear-Induced Roadblocks

If the processes, tools, and methods are consistent across industries and product lines, then so too are the fears associated with partnerships within your organization. These fears are the first real internal speed bumps you will face when starting down the road to a partnership. Fears are raised by everyone from the CEO to the research engineer and involve every functional department: marketing, product development, operations, and financial management. Before you can get the go-ahead to move forward with a partnership, it's important to address each person's concern in turn.

During the PPO identification process, fear raised by the *executive management* board and other strategic thinkers within your organization stems from the established market position, reputation, and partner history of the PPO. Once a PPO has been identified, your own *alliance manager* is concerned about the size, breadth, complexity, and dynamics of penetrating the PPO. As talks progress into the product validation due-diligence process, your *product, research,* or *technical team* raises issues about your organization's ability to trust, manage, and protect its intellectual property. Upon completion, your *financial manager* expresses fears associated with a PPO's negotiation tactics, agreement, and financial disclosure due-diligence process. Finally, when the partner agreement is concluded and signed, the *business development manager* responsible for transitioning the new relationship into a successful, revenue producing program has concerns about the ability of the PPO to execute against plan, the procedure for handling conflicts, and even the methods for measuring the program's success.

How do you handle all the concerns, fears, and anxiety? Dan Wormenhoven, CEO of Network Appliance Corporation and one of *BusinessWeek* magazine's top 25 CEOs in the United States in 2001, says you need to "isolate and parse the major concerns into smaller issues that can be solved." Once this has been done, "The issue simply disappears and the real business of partnerships can get done."

Executive Management's Fears

According to Wormenhoven, one of the primary issues resolved at the executive level is the relative presence, size, and strength of a market leader compared to your own firm. While the reality of partnership failure doesn't rest on the size or industry leadership position of the partner per se, the myth itself is hard to shake. Visions of a time-consuming endeavor with an unresponsive organization dissuades many from pursuing even an initial conversation.

Yet much of this fear rests on the perception of "low return from a high-effort/high-cost partnership development cause," explains Wormenhoven. "The real concern of the executive management team is whether or not the return from the partnership is going to be exponential or merely incremental." In short, the question is whether approaching a dominant company is worth the effort, and how to make the determination before the first foot has been put forward.

You can easily address this fear by identifying the business case supporting the potential partner opportunity. A business manager who can lead his team to a five-year, 87 percent compound annual growth rate is going to look for indicators that the alliance team has done its homework. "In addition to how much money is at stake (how much we will lose if we don't have the partnership), I and the other executive managers want to know how and when they are going to realize a return from the partnership. The risk analysis results can be weighed at either the executive management or board level depending on the partner."

Far more disconcerting than the size of an organization is the ability to identify and convey the best time to approach a PPO. If you approach a PPO too early in your company cycle, you run the risk of outpacing your personnel and financial resources, thereby imploding your organization.

This executive management fear will permeate the organization without a defined partner development timeline articulating milestones, resources, and dependencies. "A lot of alliance managers stop just long enough to consider the positive effects of a partnership, but not nearly long enough to identify the negative implications on the functional departments that must support the partnership," explained Wormenhoven. This causes unnecessary doubt and anxiety from the management team. Upon developing the road map, you not only gain verbal support for your efforts, you also completely eliminate the risk of outrunning your own resources. The executive level has the responsibility to appropriate the financial needs of each department within the organization. Armed with what will be expected when and by what groups allows the team early visibility necessary for budgeting purposes.

The last executive management concern centers on the ability of an "industry giant" to influence your company's market or product focus. This fear occurs when you are presented with a "new market segment" that could be pursued jointly with the PPO. These opportunities both flatter the ego (we are so great the PPO wants to partner with us to attack a new market) and the pocketbook (and the PPO will give us $10 million in joint development dollars!).

While these opportunities are tempting in the short term, the slight diversionary crack in your market strategy becomes a chasm of grand proportions. With a partner development road map as your guide, you will be less susceptible to corporate course changes, simultaneously allaying the executive concern of defocused efforts.

Alliance Managers' Fears

Few individuals take the time to build a sound business case and package it with a red bow. It's more about the relevance of an idea or a product to the potential partner presented in a short, clear, and concise manner. Far too many alliance managers fear that if their own partnership business case is less than a 20-page document, it will give the wrong impression. This couldn't be further from the truth. Large companies are built on ideas, innovation, and a keen ability to grasp new opportunities, make decisions quickly, and execute them. The potential partner that will understand and incorporate a straightforward approach is the one to stand out among the pile of other potential partners.

Ran Slaten, a serial entrepreneur with over 35 years as a CEO of small companies behind him, felt his present service offerings as a painting contracting firm would be unappealing to a potential partner— Home Depot. He had put together a seminar series on tips and techniques for painting in the arid region of northern California and believed this to be of value to consumers and the trade alike. But he feared he had not built a formal business case strong enough to support his conviction that his firm should be hired to teach these special in-store seminars (as opposed to Home Depot's internal team creating such a program). Individuals with great partnership ideas rarely follow through because of the fear that their small business isn't good enough for a "real company." "Real" in most cases is defined as a mid- or large-size organization as opposed to quality, service, or product offerings.

Yet Slaten's perception was incorrect. Companies like Home Depot have gained a leadership position by just such informal partnering. The majority of partnerships I've created over the past decade have started with an eight-paragraph, one-and-a-half-page document, not a 25-page proposal. Most decision makers have to use some mechanism to weed out the interesting from the dull, and fast. Lack of time, pressure to perform, or competitive threats all push decision makers at large firms to conduct business expeditiously. A concise tool such as a 2-page document is going to state the partner objective, business opportunity, details of the potential partnership, dependencies, and ultimate competitive advantage for both parties. This is considered much more meaningful than a bound document full of marketing fluff and product literature.

Remember, innovators are the oxygen larger organizations require to sustain their life support system. So if you are approaching a PPO for the first time, start simple, start small, and don't be intimidated. Many great partnerships have modest beginnings.

Alliance Managers' Fears of Divulging Too Much   Alliance managers invariably believe that secret corporate strategies are given away by responding to a question the wrong way. The fear of giving away the company direction superglues lips together so that they never do open up. No communication, no information exchange, no substantive discussions, no relationship.

This fear can be addressed by signing a *nondisclosure agreement* (NDA). An NDA is intended to place a layer of secrecy on the content of the talks with the PPO. Believe it or not, many companies have conversations with potential partners without an NDA in place. These tend to be the stories that end up in the media, and the bigger company is usually portrayed as the monster who pushed around the little guy to get the information it wanted.

Nearly 100 percent of the time, the partnership discussions or product reviews were held without a nondisclosure agreement. The most frequent victim was the inexperienced alliance manager. Caught in a halo effect of flattery after having received a call from the PPO's head honcho, the discussion led to an outpouring of proprietary information. It is an unfortunate situation that is largely preventable.

Phillip Benz, formerly vice president of marketing and sales for Instromedix and now holding the same position for medical equipment manufacturer Advanced Vascular Dynamics, has created over a dozen complex joint development, sales, and marketing agreements. He believes the key to success for alliance managers is to "seep only enough information required by the potential partner to answer the question." Too often marketing, sales, and even product development managers are apt to divulge more information than necessary while still in the throes of wanting to share all the goodness their product or firm can offer. This desire needs to be tempered with caution.

This may seem like common sense, yet many bright entrepreneurs want to "change the world" says Steve Edmiston, cofounder of Front Porch Classics. A litigation lawyer by training, Edmiston jumped ship to create coffee table board games. Edmiston learned the hard way that a potential partner can also be a competitor with only a slight change in market focus. Entrepreneurs endowed with equal parts vision, passion, and enthusiasm are always open to the potential opportunities of tomorrow. However, he advises "while it may be hard to lasso your desire to express your plans for the future, it's going to be required until an agreement is in place and the partnership has had time to produce tangible results."

Alliance Managers' Fears of The Fatal Mistake   The fear of The Fatal Mistake is in fact one of the more predominant and hard-to-eliminate fears associated with partner development. Perhaps one too many partnership sob stories have identified "the single mistake" responsible for taking a company down. My belief is that the fable of a single fatal mistake is just that—a fable. More likely, a series of mistakes were made without correction.

Partner development practitioners like me who do nothing but create alliances often use the phrase *historical precedence*. Most commonly, they use it when trying to determine if a PPO has entered into a similar partnership in the past akin to what is trying to be created today. The purpose of the exercise is to use the information to predict the future. The result is considered to be the *predictable outcome* of an intended partnership. If you are familiar with a case of partnership failure, be sure to investigate the situation as thoroughly as possible, and then look for other relevant examples of partnership history with the same target partner. Conducting this due-diligence check will likely answer your questions while providing useful insights and ideas.

Management's Fears of the Product Validation Process

The product validation process is the most crucial phase of the partnership development. This is the stage in which your product and any of the potential partner's products are tested in order to validate that they operate as intended. Unfortunately, it is also the most misunderstood and feared aspect of the partnership cycle, due to the fact that the process is structured differently from company to company. Also, the larger of the two organizations has the luxury of determining where and when the product testing will be performed. This places the smaller of the two firms at a serious disadvantage: The smaller firm doesn't control the testing environment and therefore cannot ensure the testing process or results. Worse, this uneven playing field sets up a potentially unfavorable scenario for future partnership negotiation.

During the course of the product testing, fears of product theft arise, as do concerns over excessive costs associated with supporting a testing environment out of one's own office. If your product is dependent in some way on the potential partner's product, it's possible that an error on their side will affect the performance of your own product.

You can address the technical team's fears of testing the product by managing the due-diligence process. If a due-diligence process does not exist, you need to participate in the development of the process and criteria. Furthermore, the checklist of what will be tested, and where and by whom, is largely in your control. If product evaluation is to be conducted on the PPO's premises, you can provide a product with limited functionality, or you can be on-site during the evaluations. If this is not acceptable, it's almost always possible to hire an independent third-party organization to conduct the testing. In this way, product confidentiality is guaranteed, and the published results are unbiased. Either conducting the evaluation on-site or with a third party controls the costs of the effort as well, eliminating concern that testing expenses will be out of control.

Finance Managers' Fears

When it comes time to structure, negotiate, and close a partnership agreement, the financial manager is going to need to know the history and reputation of the potential partner. It's also reasonable for the financial manager to request evidence of other partnerships negotiated and closed with the PPO.

These requests stem from the desire to understand and prepare for the worst-case negotiation environment. Hardball tactics are associated with some companies more than others. Consider, for example, America Online. National publications such as *Fortune* and *BusinessWeek* have cited AOL's partnership management team for use of hardball, white-knuckle tactics. Such tactics have included changing prices and, more importantly, endless negotiations, shifting of primary issues, and late-stage changes in the agreement. All of this reportedly done in an effort to unsettle the (usually smaller) partner into bending to AOL's terms and conditions. One CEO likened going through this agreement process to being put through an old-fashioned wringer washing machine: He came out flat and nearly broke.

My own entrepreneurial father subscribed to the principle of price and terms. He was willing to negotiate anything under the condition that his price was traded for the partner's terms, or vice versa. His intent was to ensure fairness on both accounts. Mark Anderson, CEO of Anderson Hay and Grain, has been applying this principle for the last 15 years, and his father did so for 35 years before him. As a grower, harvester, and distributor of grain products, Anderson has grown from $5 million to over $100 million in 2002 under Mark Anderson's tutelage. The bulk of this growth is due to a handful of marketing and distribution partnerships.

Phillip Benz of Advanced Vascular Dynamics cautions that fairness doesn't mean the negotiations must lack intensity:

> *If the spirit of the negotiation is not conducted with the right intent of profit, fairness, and longevity, it's a sign that the partnership isn't going to stand the test of time. . . . I'm one of the most aggressive negotiators I've come across, but that doesn't mean I'm going to ask for an unfair price. Everyone has a final number. It's up to me to determine what that is and how I present it to the other side. The key to successful negotiation and deal closure rests on both sides reaching a point of candor about the core terms and conditions early on. How these terms and conditions are balanced with price can always be worked out if the intent is aligned.*

Once the core terms and conditions have been agreed to, the process accelerates. In negotiating, setting expectations is critical, and the negotiator—be it the financial manager or alliance manager—can eliminate the fear surrounding negotiation if expectations are established at the outset. For example, cash-oriented incentives and penalties should be addressed in the plan, well before they are stipulated in the financial agreement. After such thorough groundwork, the actual negotiating of an agreement is almost a nonissue. Phillip Benz starts planting the seeds of the price he wants during the product evaluation process, "as soon as we know the products work and we have created supporting numbers of product projections. If I do that with the right people, word spreads, and by the time I'm at the table, we are working with a realistic set of starting points. This cuts down on the usual back-and-forth maneuvering and ensures a more straightforward conversation that deals with the issues of substance as opposed to positioning."

Both Benz and Anderson agree that the alliance manager responsible for creating the partnership has more do to with successful contract negotiation than the financial manager who constructs the agreement. A partnership plan can eliminate the financial manager's concern that the partnership financial requirements will outstrip available funds.

Business Development Managers' Fears

In sufficiently large companies, the day-to-day management of the partnership will be assigned to an alliance or business development manager. This individual is going to have anxieties about delivering on the promise of the alliance and meeting the initial partnership objectives, as well as fears about the mesh of partners' culture and methods of working. Ultimately, the business development manager will want to feel confident in the ability of his or her company to respond and react to the results (positive or negative) of the partnership.

These fears can be quickly and easily addressed by providing the business development manager the history of the partnership, the long-term plan, the background culture of the engagement (your experience), and the outcome of the negotiation process (the agreement). This four-fold view is grounded in how the partnership supports the overarching partner goals, which in turn supports the objectives of the corporation. Educated with this perspective, the alliance or business development manager should know the value and relative importance of the partnership to the company.

Turning the Negative Attitudes into Positive Attitudes

Fear serves the true purpose of injecting caution into business practices. With proper planning and forethought, most fears, concerns, and doubts about a potential partnership are removed. Appropriately set expectations further reduce anxiety and hesitation on the part of those supporting partnership development efforts. Anticipating and addressing fears can transform the once-negative energy into efforts conducted with a positive and constructive attitude.

If anyone on your supporting team is experiencing fear-induced symptoms, you should assess the source of the fear and proactively deal with it. Once you have put to rest all the typical fears, you will be well on your way to building the first major component of your alliance strategy and completing the AllianceMapping model.

4

AllianceMapping

CHAPTER HIGHLIGHTS

- *Dissecting the AllianceMapping cycle*
- *AllianceMapping for product-based firms*
- *AllianceMapping for service-based firms*
- *Fixing imperfect alliances*

Partnerships as Strategic Warfare

IT'S BEEN SAID THAT "time is the greatest innovator." This statement certainly applies when countries are looking to extend their dominance. Evidence of this can also be seen in the tools employed to gain advantage in the corporate landscape of that time—the battlefield.

During the fourth and fifth centuries, a revolution occurred in the character of the Roman armies and warfare tactics. During one particular battle, the Romans found their infantry crushed by the German cavalry. The Romans quickly adopted this strategy and improved upon it by placing groups of mobile cavalry units around their territories. No longer residing at the Roman headquarters until a battle was a foot, the *comitatenses*, or mobile army, was dispatched at the direction of the emperor. By the sixth century, Roman victories were again commonplace.

A thousand years later, warfare was again revolutionized, this time by the Swiss pikemen and the English archers. During the fourteenth and fifteenth centuries these countries demonstrated innovations that effectively thwarted the opponent's cavalry. Hand-to-hand contact was replaced with long-range weapons and focused tactics that enabled warriors to selectively pick off their targets.

Over the course of history, markets have been created and maintained through the use of force of one kind or another. In a civilized society, the weapons used to protect against a business adversary are competitive products and good financial and legal advisors. Weapons are not objects of steel and wood but pieces of paper. Innovation is not focused on the physical elimination of the enemy but is applied to achieving more market share, faster and more profitably.

In this environment, partnerships are a form of strategic warfare. Business objectives are set and partner strategies are designed to attain them. The tools used to execute the tactics are creatively designed agreements. Yet as we have learned from the market leaders of old, strategies and tools must continue to evolve to meet the opponents' new strategies and tools. Partnerships of yesterday are not going to meet the market requirements of today, nor will they meet the requirements of tomorrow. To achieve success, partner strategies require innovation.

The Second Priority

Ask any executive of a large company about the company's partner strategy and you will probably hear that the company has a "partner model designed to fulfill specific requirements of company growth." That's exactly what CEO Dan Wormenhoven of Network Appliance said when asked about the partner planning process. Each partner was carefully chosen to get a job done and supply a specific function within the business.

Contrast this with the process followed by Phillip Benz, vice president of Advanced Vascular Dynamics, a classic small business with less than $25 million in sales. He admits that the process to creating even his most profitable partnership was very informal. "I'd like to say it was on purpose and it worked out as I planned it, but it was actually somewhere between rigorous planning and dumb luck."

If you ask an executive of a company with revenues of less than $25 million the same question, you will likely hear a very different answer. "Pretty ad hoc," is what Mitch Mounger of Sunrise Identity, a manufacturer of branded apparel and specialty products said about his firm's partner strategy. And yet even Mounger was able to craft a very successful partnership.

These varied experiences exemplify just how wide the chasm of partner planning and development is between the largest and smallest of firms. While large companies make long-term strategic business plans, those further down the financial food chain veer toward common sense and gut feelings. While Benz might like to have the time to plan out every partnership, and Mounger acknowledges that he probably should have conducted more due-diligence product reviews, these lofty goals were not realized. When the demands of keeping up sales without sacrificing customer satisfaction are constant worries, most executives of small and midsize businesses acknowledge that planning partnerships are a second priority. What's more, even in a robust economy, CEOs are reluctant to spend for outside expertise on a partner development planning process when the same money could be spent on another sales representative.

However, this does not have to be the case. While few companies are endowed with the luxury of hiring dedicated alliance managers or spending months planning a partner strategy, these time and money constraints are no longer impediments to partner development. So how do you start the process of figuring out your partner model when you lack the background, expertise, or financial support to create your most strategic weapon? You start with the first and most important cornerstone of partner development: AllianceMapping.

AllianceMapping Defined

AllianceMapping is the name of a model that every organization can use to pinpoint the right partner for any given stage in its life cycle. If this is done correctly, the organization can then identify the predictable outcomes, resource requirements, associated risks, and revenue projections for the partnership. What this ultimately means is that each organization can create a long-term strategic partnership road map, just as the big firms do.

AllianceMapping helps you answer the most basic questions at the outset of the partner development cycle:

- Who would want to partner with my company?
- Is my business at a stage in which I should consider a partnership?
- What would a partnership require from my firm in terms of money and time?
- Is there a way I can tell if a PPO will be interested before I spend time on creating the partnership?
- Is there a way to figure out a fluid partner road map that matches my company's expected growth?
- How will I know when my existing partners stop benefiting me?

The AllianceMapping Equation

The best business models are those that appear extremely simple and yet deliver incredibly powerful results. This is true with AllianceMapping. In this model, you will identify three things: the state of your product, the state of capital financing, and the desired partnership objectives. If these three aspects are aligned, then you know your partnership model has a solid chance of succeeding. You can then establish a path of progression for the partner development cycle (Figure 4–1).

The starting point is analyzing the status of your company and of its product(s), which are the main focus of any potential partner. This analysis is critical to the success of the AllianceMapping model, as your firm will be appealing to some partners when your company or product is at one stage, and completely unappealing to those partners when it is in another. The possible evolutionary stages are the same as the five traditional product development stages. They are as follows:

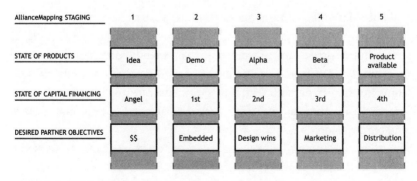

AllianceMapping STAGING	1	2	3	4	5
STATE OF PRODUCTS	Idea	Demo	Alpha	Beta	Product available
STATE OF CAPITAL FINANCING	Angel	1st	2nd	3rd	4th
DESIRED PARTNER OBJECTIVES	$$	Embedded	Design wins	Marketing	Distribution

Figure 4–1 AllianceMapping Model for Product-Based Firms

- Stage 1: Idea
- Stage 2: Demo
- Stage 3: Alpha
- Stage 4: Beta
- Stage 5: Product available

The second step of AllianceMapping validates the financial status of your company. For privately held firms, this is parsed into formal funding rounds. If your company is self-funded, then you simply assess the amount of discretionary capital available for partnership programs.

The last step of AllianceMapping is to identify your partnership objectives. Use the partnership types described in Chapter 2 to guide you in formulating your partnership objectives. Focus on which area of your business can be augmented or which area needs to cut its costs. Often, the answer will be that your business needs help in more than one area and that you will need to create more than one partnership.

Creating Your AllianceMap

Now that you understand the three components of the model, it's time to map the alliance best suited for your organization. Using the illustration in Figure 4–1, circle the three criteria that most accurately represent your firm. Now draw a line that connects the three circles.

You have thus identified whether or not you have a high chance of succeeding in creating your desired partnership. If the line is straight, you can feel confident that you are in the top 5 percent of companies pursuing a partnership with all the attributes necessary to make the partnership happen. Your partnership objectives are reasonable for the state of your product and the financial situation of your company. This is the first, best type of company other firms seek in terms of targeting their own potential partners.

On the other hand, if your line is more reminiscent of a jagged connect the dots puzzle, don't be surprised or discouraged. The majority of companies start out with misaligned or unrealistic expectations. You need to focus on why the graph looks like *geographically dispersed circles* and try to identify a way to realign the attributes. By spending important time thinking through your business plan, you will essentially be creating a new road map for your business, as well as a road map to a potential partnership.

AllianceMapping can be used to identify, plan, and act on the objectives, strategies, and partner development tactics for any business. When the exercise is about reducing risk, increasing return, and following a logical and focused growth course, no company should be dissuaded from using AllianceMapping. The following examples are just snapshots of how AllianceMapping aligned companies in very different industries and business models. Yet within minutes, the AllianceMapping exercise identified if the partnerships were going to work.

Mike Walsh's executive management team at Actify, a design-sharing solutions manufacturer, epitomizes the AllianceMapping model. His team has used AllianceMapping not only to plan out his company's partnership road map for today but for the long term as well. For example, Actify's marketing partnership is 12 to 18 months out on the partner development life cycle given the growth plan of customers, funding, and infrastructure. Walsh and his team know that while they are focused on creating OEM relationships today, in 18 months, sales from these partnerships will have brought the company to a point at which it can sustain a direct sales force. This means Actify knows where it is going and how it will get there. The company also knows that a sales and distribution partnership will take about 6 months to create and another 6 months to roll out to the field. So instead of waiting until the 17th month, the company will have to determine *who* will be its distribution partner in 5 months. This knowledge allows the team to allocate budgets and personnel accordingly.

Back in 1996, Christian Karr of Espresso Connection had no money, no means of outside capital financing, no land on which to place a coffee cart, and no means to create visibility. Espresso Connection is a textbook example of how to use AllianceMapping from the initial company life-cycle stages.

Espresso Connection required idea validation and additional dollars to bring its product to market. With no more than an idea and a mocked-up prototype, Karr approached a provider of coffee, Seattle's Best Coffee, to aid his company in both the design of this final product and to OEM their coffee beans. In this way, Karr propelled Espresso Connection from stage 1 to stage 2.

In parallel, Karr was planning out the growth stages and the necessary partners to bridge the gap between growth periods. Once Espresso Connection was in stage 2, he had a product that could be tested and a resident OEM agreement with an established brand, and he was ready to move to stage 3, which was to test the first mobile coffee stand. To determine if the business model would be a financial success, Karr had to create a facilities partnership with zero money out. He also needed to create awareness for his new stand as soon as it was ready. Simultaneously, Karr created the facilities partnership for his first location and then enacted a new marketing agreement with Seattle's Best Coffee.

While the time between stages from stage 1 through stage 4 was a matter of weeks and months, the time between stages 4 and 5 was about 18 months. Karr maintained a vision of distributing the Espresso Connection products through a partner channel, but he could not explore this opportunity until his initial business model was proven. In the meantime, Karr identified the right distribution partners for his product line, and he is now in the process of creating partners that can extend his product line to the masses.

AllianceMapping for Product-Based Firms

In the next examples, see if you can identify patterns or similarities in the situations. Consider the risks faced by each firm and how it chose to eliminate the risks.

Sunstream Corporation provides a great example of smart partnership development. Ken Hey, Sunstream's CEO, initially created a manufacturing partnership when the company was in stage 4 (shipping) of its boat manufacturing cycle. Incorporated at that stage, the partnership saved capital costs and risks associated with hiring full-time personnel. The second partnership Sunstream created was during stage 1, when it was looking for innovative design and development ideas. This engineering agreement aided the development of a second generation of product, again without costing Sunstream initial or long-term capital. Each relationship was created at a specific point in Sunstream's life cycle.

In this process, Sunstream bridged the gap from stage 2 to 3 and 4 through its manufacturing and engineering partnership. When it was ready to move to stage 5, Hey and his team wisely sought a marketing and sales relationship. With an eye on an aligned target market, Sunstream approached Cobalt Boats. The partnership value proposition that Sunstream proposed included bundling a sale of a Cobalt boat with a hydraulic boat lift from Sunstream. Ken was convinced that Cobalt dealers would sell more boats if consumers were able to have an easier time launching and docking the boats. The risk to Cobalt dealers would be low, and Sunstream committed to having a sales representative train each local dealer. The same representative would also train each new customer who purchased the boat lift.

The AllianceMapping of Sunstream's growth is another perfect example of logical partnership progression. At each stage, the state of the product, funding, and the partnership desired matched the partnership created. The value proposition resonated with Cobalt because it wanted to improve the customer experience as a means of differentiation.

The results of the stage 5 partnership are impressive. Although starting small, with just a few local dealerships (in an informal or verbal contract), within two years the partnership terms extended nationally to a high percentage of Cobalt's 60 dealers. In terms of measured success, customer satisfaction rates skyrocketed as boat owners reported to the Cobalt dealers that they were using their boat two to three times as often because of the new boat lift. Boat owners referred an average of two customers per year that converted into sales, and they said they made such referrals because of the ease of using the boat lift supplied by Sunstream. If this weren't enough, boat owners were found to trade in their own boats more frequently in order to move up in boat size— again, due to boating more often as a direct result of the ease of the boat lift. All of this translated into very real and measurable dollars to the Cobalt dealer and the Sunstream representative. According to Hey, the best part about this particular agreement was that the time to creating revenue from the first phone call was 60 days.

In 2001, an apex of the relationship was achieved when Cobalt invited Sunstream to debut Sunstream's new floating boat lift at the Cobalt national dealer conference by lifting a Cobalt boat in and out of a huge water-filled tank. With the success of the marketing and sales partnership, the two companies are now working on a joint development agreement for the next generation of products. According to Hey, Cobalt desires to "open up its market from lake boats to all boats, but what they have asked is for Sunstream to share any innovative ideas for their boat design." This is a first for Cobalt as well as for Sunstream. "We have a substantial engineering department full of creative designers coming up with revolutionary concepts one after the other, and now we have an immediate outlet to get these concepts into the market," beamed Hey.

A second example is Laurie Erickson's firm, The Finest Accessories (TFA), which creates high-end hair clips that are sold in Nordstrom's, Bloomingdales, and other fashionable stores. The firm experienced triple-digit growth to become a $3 million business in just a few years. The company's partnerships with suppliers and manufacturers followed a nearly identical course as that of Sunstream.

The TFA experience differed when Erickson was approached by cellular phone giant Motorola's products accessories division. In this unique scenario, the larger company provided TFA a value proposition to design and manufacture cellular phone faceplates. The faceplates would then be purchased by Motorola and assembled onto their cell phones. While this opportunity posed a diversification from its core business, TFA would realize a new revenue stream with minimal change in its business model. In addition to differentiating its product line, Motorola would gain innovation without the cost of employing a non-core business process.

TFA's AllianceMap for Motorola aligned perfectly as a joint development partner. In the case of TFA, this manifests itself in an alignment with stage 3 (testing). TFA created an early prototype within days of its first meeting with the Motorola team. Motorola liked the prototype and agreed to pay for the design and development work. Motorola's desired partnership included exclusivity in using the designs, but it did not call for ownership of the designs themselves. TFA agreed to those terms and maintains both the licensing and copyright ownership of the designs.

Because this partnership includes Motorola's purchasing of the completed faceplates from TFA, the relationship does not extend to stage 4 or 5. Rather, Motorola itself manages the marketing and distribution of the products as opposed to TFA. Erickson has found that there are benefits of a partnership limited to research, design, and development: "Our portion is fun, short, and very profitable." The time to create the relationship from the first phone call to revenue dollar 1 was nine months.

Another good example is the Arlen Ness company, a $10 million manufacturer of motorcycle products. In its 10 years in business, the company had reached a plateau. Beginning as a high-end specialty motorcycle manufacturer, it continued to grow through diversifying its product line to include motorcycle clothes and equipment. After an assessment of target consumers, Ness decided it needed to work with a leader in another field to jointly produce products that would take advantage of its technology and expertise in the motorcycle arena.

In this case, Ness decided to propose a partnership with Polaris Corporation, an organization that consumers associated closely with affordable products. Best known for its line of snowmobiles, Polaris had been attempting to diversify its own product line but with little success. Polaris thus agreed to a partnership with Ness. The objective of both firms was to differentiate their product lines in mature markets, while generating interest and increased sales.

The companies formed a joint development agreement to produce a line of cobranded motorcycles. These custom-built street bikes are now sold under the name Arlen Ness Polaris. While Ness custom-made bikes regularly sell for over $100,000 and are driven by ex-presidents, celebrities, and athletes, the Arlen Ness Polaris branded bike that is now available to the general public attracts a tremendous amount of attention for both firms.

The AllianceMap for Ness and Polaris is interesting. Their relationship evolved with the need to expand their product lines. The companies aligned at each stage of AllianceMapping, starting in stage 1 (idea) and going all the way through stage 5 (product availability). While Ness gained marketing, distribution, and sales efforts, Polaris was able to be the first company to bring an authorized Ness product to the general market.

Let's look at what makes this evolution unique. At the first stage, Ness had created an idea for a mass-produced line of bikes, but the company lacked the distribution channel. Ness was also stymied by its inability to diversify. Both needs were met by Polaris. When the product reached testing and completion, Polaris provided the licensing rights and national marketing power, and it pushed the bikes to market through its distribution channel.

AllianceMapping for Service-Based Firms

Service providers such as consultants, real estate agents, and other professionals rely on their own expertise to create revenue. A service is an "intangible product," and it is harder to quantify for purposes of assessing company growth. As a result, partnerships between service-to-service or service-to-product businesses tend to be oriented toward marketing and sales initiatives as opposed to new product development.

Service-based marketing and sales partnerships can be less formal than joint development or distribution partnerships, but they are nevertheless much more than simple referrals. Referrals do not constitute a true partnership. They are simply one aspect of conducting business with another individual or organization so as to aid customers of the referring company. Referrals don't take the money, time, effort, or energy that are invested in the game of partnerships. As a result, referrals are convenient, but they cannot be depended upon to drive a predictable amount of revenue every month, quarter, or year.

In contrast, marketing and sales partnerships between service companies percolate through awareness creation and lead generation, personnel training, services diversification, and customer fulfillment. Through these partnerships, service providers are sharing an existing or intended customer base with a partner so as to increase customer loyalty, satisfaction, and/or revenue to both firms. In a flat or downturned economy, customer loyalty is paramount in maintaining margins and profitability. Professionals who consistently deliver innovative and timely services that their customers truly need and value will earn the loyalty of those customers.

The AllianceMapping Model for Service-Based Firms

Service companies utilize a slightly modified AllianceMapping model to identify and validate the most appropriate partnership. In the services model, the state of the products and capital financing is different while the type of partnership is consistent with the products model (Figure 4–2).

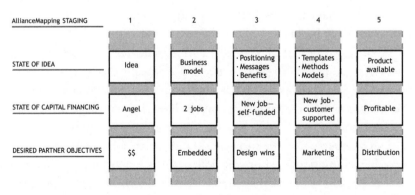

AllianceMapping STAGING	1	2	3	4	5
STATE OF IDEA	Idea	Business model	· Positioning · Messages · Benefits	· Templates · Methods · Models	Product available
STATE OF CAPITAL FINANCING	Angel	2 jobs	New job—self-funded	New job-customer supported	Profitable
DESIRED PARTNER OBJECTIVES	$$	Embedded	Design wins	Marketing	Distribution

Figure 4–2   AllianceMapping for Service-Based Companies

Since many service firms start out as sole proprietorships, I've included these small firms to show the magnitude of the effect a partnership can have on a business. For example, like many independent consultants, forty-two-year old Joan Mara had an advanced college degree and a long history of expertise in the field of organizational training and behavior. To differentiate her business, Mara focused on facilitating management meetings, aiding executives during times of planning and conflict alike.

Mara quickly realized she could grow the company through word of mouth, but exponential growth would be possible only through a smart partnership. She approached the Young Entrepreneurs' Organization (YEO), an international forum established to aid entrepreneurs forty years old and younger, to gain perspective and knowledge from their unique peer group. While the YEO was clearly succeeding as an organization, as evidenced in its strong membership of 2000 people and its presence in nearly 40 countries, the members were complaining that the quality of the forum discussions could be better. Mara provided a value proposition that included the development of a process for interpersonal communication. Not only would she create a process specifically tailored to this community but she would also train YEO forums and facilitate meetings.

Mara had never before created a partnership. This didn't stop her, however, from gaining a marketing partnership with the YEO. Within a year of creating the partnership, developing the tools and training the members, membership satisfaction increased dramatically. This directly reduced the rate of member attrition while simultaneously increasing the membership. For Mara, the success of her program with the YEO led to local and national requests from individual chapters for her forums, which she could provide without spending money on marketing and advertising her business.

Mara's AllianceMap is classic of a services firm in the fourth stage of development (marketing). Mara needed to actually create processes for communication, templates for meeting management, and new methods to ensure optimal communication. While she was developing this information at her new company, she was supporting the business through other customer projects. Mara's partnership with the YEO cost her nothing in hard or soft dollars. Most important, this service-based marketing partnership was created quickly. In Mara's case, the time to create the relationship from the first phone call to realizing the first dollar of revenue was only 45 days.

Partnerships among Professional Services Providers

Legal, insurance, and accounting firms have tremendous opportunities to partner with one another to surround and capture target markets. A good example is a relationship that began with a 50-person law firm and an 18-person insurance brokerage firm located in the same northwest city.

Unbeknownst to either firm, each had a target market of small companies between 50 and 100 employees, and each focused on one particular area of expertise: corporate liability with regard to workers' discrimination and harassment claims. The insurance company wanted to prevent client claims from increasing. The law firm was interested in educating its clients on the risks, processes, and programs that would help reduce or eliminate potentially damaging situations.

To address this situation, each firm had created free services for its client base. The insurance company had produced a training program for educating its clients, leaving the responsibility for handling the training with the client. The law firm had tried a different approach. One of the partners specializing in employee-related litigation had created a two-hour management seminar that was given by the firm at no charge to its clients. Each program was beneficial but did not produce revenue for either company. Instead, it reduced risks and potential litigation costs and associated premium increases.

Once I put the firms in touch with one another, the partnership opportunity was obvious. Through a formal marketing and sales partnership, the two programs would be combined into one training and education program on employee discrimination. Under the agreement, each firm would promote the program to its respective client base. Sales representatives from the insurance company and the partners in the law firm underwent formal training on the benefits, components, and pricing of the program. Sales targets were given to each firm, with a goal of one new program sale per week. Commission would be paid to the sales representative and the revenue split between the two firms.

In this particular case, the AllianceMapping model was completed and determined at stage 4. Creating the partnership enabled the templates, tools, and models to be leveraged and distributed in a stream-lined fashion. Nominal effort was required to combine the programs and distribute them to market. Now that both firms are in stage 5, the distribution model could be easily modified for additional partners. Intellectual property, client ownership, and revenue-sharing issues were easily and quickly addressed. The time from the initial conversation to program implementation was less than 60 days.

Partnering a Product-Based Firm with a Service-Based Firm

It is very common to find a company providing services in partnership with a company delivering products to deliver a complete solution to the market. In this case, the AllianceMapping model follows the original product formula. The difference is noted in the manifestation of how a service-based product is brought to market as opposed to a physical product. For service-based firms, ideas transform into documents and marketing materials that make up the physical product. One example is a partnership created between The Nature Conservancy, a service-based company, and giant Princess Cruise Lines. The Nature Conservancy (TNC), a 3000-person multinational nonprofit, began purchasing land 50 years ago in an effort to preserve natural habitats. Its business model changed when a new management team came onboard in 1999. The new team viewed its land purchases as "ecoregions" with needs unique to the area, climate, and other topographical elements, as opposed to simple blocks of unprotected lands. TNC needed its partnership model to evolve to one that would provide a forum to educate the public on this approach. At the same time, donations to many nonprofit environmental groups were decreasing, and TNC was worried that its core funding would diminish if it changed course.

TNC reviewed the characteristics of its individual contributors—their interests, habits, and spending traits. The result of this exercise was a decision to combine awareness and education with recreational travel. TNC approached Princess Cruise Lines with a value proposition to loan its environmental, archeological, and history experts to give seminars on cruises specifically designed for TNC potential contributors. In return, Princess Cruise Lines would market and manage the cruises.

Both organizations would monetarily benefit from travelers' experiencing a much more satisfying cruise.

Princess Cruise Lines was in AllianceMapping stage 5. Its product was complete, and its finances were assured, and it was looking for a means to develop a new client base. This meant distributing its cruise line revenue opportunities to the well-healed traveler. The Nature Conservancy was in stage 4. It had the marketing templates, models, and positioning for a new type of service, but it needed a marketing venue in which to create awareness and demand for its programs. The partnership would help both, as each organization would extend into a slightly new consumer demographic profile while increasing the satisfaction of existing customers.

To bridge the gap between stages, Princess Cruise Lines had to work with TNC on customizing the program service offerings, such as the brochures, messaging, and campaign particulars. To take advantage of the Princess Cruise Lines opportunity, TNC needed to work with Princess to complete the marketing materials, line up experts for specific cruises, and make the program publicly available.

The results of this joint development and marketing agreement helped the partners meet their goals. Additionally, Princess Cruise Lines gained a tremendous advantage being associated with such a prestigious organization. At the same time, TNC reached an audience that would have been otherwise impossible to penetrate due to limited funding available for mass direct-mail and advertising campaigns to promote new programs.

According to Steve Volkers, vice president of business development for The Nature Conservancy, it took approximately a year from the first phone call to realizing revenue from the partnership.

Realignment Strategies

Paramount to the capacity of the partnership to provide value to your organization is attaining the correct alignment of your firm and the potential partner organization. Thus far, I've provided examples of companies aligned with potential partners either by luck or by plan. Yet a large number of firms are not going to be aligned with their potential partner organizations. It's important to understand why this occurs and how the alignment can be corrected before partnerships are pursued.

Common Misalignments

One adage I've always followed in my personal life is to never grocery shop when I'm hungry. I buy too much food that I never eat and, in the process, blow my grocery budget out the door. Ultimately my fridge is full of expensive products that eventually rot before I ever have the opportunity to make a meal.

So is the nature of a partnership in which the alignment is wrong. Target partners that are premature for your company's state and growth stage are the most common reason for partnership misalignment. When a partnership is prematurely formed, it rots before either party can take advantage of its attributes.

Consider the example of a five-person firm trying to launch a new product. The first desire is to create awareness and demand for the product. This, in turn, generates sales. The strategy makes sense if the manufacturing, fulfillment, supply chain, and financial support are in place. If not, the strategy intended to stimulate market demand will do nothing more than implode the company. Staging the partnerships with the natural development of the company requires the alliance manager to exercise patience in executing against a planned road map.

Misalignment also occurs in the early stages of product development. Consider the example of a product-based firm with an alpha-stage prototype. Licensing and distribution agreements should not be pursued at this time because the product is neither finished nor tested, nor in any way ready for market delivery. Yet in the rush to the sales finish line, aggressive business development managers often appeal to partnerships oriented more toward sales than product development. This enthusiasm is easily harnessed and directed by a strong leadership team. Utilizing the partner development road map will eliminate a premature product partnership.

Lack of sufficient funding prevents many partnerships from being completed. Aligning your company's financial status with the potential partner's will eliminate the risk associated with pursuing a financially insupportable partnership. This occurs most frequently with marketing, distribution, and manufacturing partnerships.

Correcting Misaligned Partner Strategies

The best strategy for achieving success through partnerships is to utilize the AllianceMapping model. If your goals are not aligned with the state and stage of product and funding, you need only to choreograph a change in the plan to meet your goals. If two of the three components are aligned, then you can elect to change the aspect of the model that is misaligned.

Consider the example in which funding is misaligned. If the product and partnership objectives are aligned but the financial resources are not available, the partners have the option of attaining the required financial support. It is not a perfect alignment and, therefore, not a ready-made or proven partnership situation. However, it doesn't mean options are not available. You can obtain internal or external funding. Even the potential partner can be required to supply the funding.

In another common example, the offered product is not aligned with the partnership. In the example of Mara Consulting and the Young Entrepreneurs' Organization, Mara was offered a marketing partnership with YEO. According to the AllianceMapping model, at the time of the offer, she was not ready to engage in a partnership of a marketing type. She did not have the funding, product line, or support infrastructure. She easily addressed this by slowing down the partnership process until her service offerings had caught up. Mara stepped back to the product development stage, jointly created the service package, and thereby worked with YEO in a joint development capacity. As the service offering was tested and proven, the marketing agreement came to pass. The YEO was able to work within the time frame and deliverable schedule while Mara developed and delivered a quality product. This is a great example of realigning the partnership with company capabilities.

If a particularly interesting marketing or distribution partnership is on the horizon, appeal to your other partners, banks, or financial sources to fund the necessary support infrastructure. If a market opportunity is recognized, product development can be supported through a new AllianceMapping cycle as opposed to folding the opportunity into an existing product line. This support enables the financial and partnership aspects to fall in line with ease.

It is rare that a partnership opportunity cannot be aligned. It is the degree to which you are willing to work with the other aspects of the organization and its willingness to compromise and adjust its schedules that determine if an alignment is to take place. If it is not possible, strongly reconsider pursuing the relationship until the alignment is more favorable to your position.

5

Creating the Partnership Plan

CHAPTER HIGHLIGHTS

- *The five-step partnership planning process*
- *Time frame guidelines for partnership creation*
- *Matching revenue expectations with potential risks of partnerships*
- *The best ways to measure partner performance*

Guarding Your Company through Partnerships

IN ROMAN TIMES, any person considered in danger applied for special protection, and it was given by an appointed judge. Having this kind of protection was known as the *tuitio*. It is the genesis of the word *guardian*, and its use can be dated to A.D. 393. The meaning of the word evolved over the ages to apply to countries, organizations, or entities who served as a guardian to protect one entity from another.

Think of partnerships as a way of protecting a company from competitive, market, or economic threats. How you plan for these partnerships is just as important as the partnerships themselves. Therefore, you can think of your partnership plan as the *tuitio* that serves your company by protecting it against unfriendly partners.

Making Time for the Planning Stage

At today's rubber-burning pace of business, a majority of partnerships are created opportunistically, randomly, and reactively. Have you ever seen a hunter pulling a gun on a flock of birds? Half the time it's a shotgun that fires dozens of pellets in all directions. This is the world of partnership strategy today: Lots of partnerships are made, hoping that one in the bunch will pay off.

"We are 11 days away from sitting down at the negotiation table with the industry leader in our category," explained the CEO of a $40 million health food manufacturer, "and we don't even know the questions to ask." In my experience, about one in every eight companies has a partnership outline. Of these, perhaps one quarter possess an actual plan that details the objectives, targets, strategy, and expected outcome of a partnership. All the others either have not thought through the role partnerships play in their businesses or at least have not developed a strong, formalized opinion. When asked about creating a partner plan, nearly every CEO responds the same way: "I would if I had the time." This is particularly true for small- and medium-size business owners and managers.

Contrary to popular belief, creating a partnership plan doesn't require a company to take a 60-day hiatus from its activities. Semiannual and annual business planning occurs regularly at most professionally managed firms without the interruption of the business cycle. Partnership development planning should be occurring in parallel with the product, operations, engineering, and human resources planning, as it is uniquely intertwined with nearly every department.

Furthermore, partner planning is no more complex than planning for the other functional departments. In some ways, it is the opposite. The components used to form a partnership plan are easy to understand and can be accomplished by nearly anyone. Armed with the AllianceMapping results, you already have ideas about the best type of potential partnership for your company. Creating the partnership plan builds the house on top of this foundation.

Lastly, a plan reduces the risk associated with partnership development more than any other activity. Think of it as an insurance policy. Simply by going through the exercises, you have considered so many different scenarios, and your team has uncovered pitfalls and potential traps. You might even uncover other opportunities not previously identified.

This chapter identifies the four required aspects of a partnership plan. It then provides the step-by-step process for creating your own partnership strategy without having to hire outside expertise or utilize other internal resources.

The Five-Step Partnership Planning Process

Creating a partnership plan is a multistep process that can be completed in as little as a few hours and at most a few days. It starts with a clear understanding of the best potential partners and of your financial and business value proposition. Coloring the potential partnerships are the benefits, risks, time frames, and resource requirements to build and manage each one. Once the course has been mapped, the companies are approached and the partnership creation process begins.

A comprehensive partner plan occurs in these five stages:

1. Stating the objectives for the alliance group
2. Identifying and assigning values to a potential partner
3. Assessing and assigning risk associated with a potential partner
4. Determining potential revenue derived from a partner
5. Stating means of measuring the partnership(s)

Completing these five steps enables you to understand the resource requirements associated with each partnership path, as well as the overall return, simply by calculating basic costs from revenue. It will also provide a realistic and predictable outcome.

Time Frames Based on AllianceMapping

Having completed your own AllianceMap, you have an idea of the right time for partnership creation. If this is your first time creating a partnership and you are unfamiliar with how long different types of partnerships take for completion, use the guide in Table 5–1. (Note that each of the partnerships in Table 5–1 is single-faceted—that is, none includes combination partnerships with two or more aspects for which the timeline would be extended considerably.)

Table 5–1 Partnership Creation Timeline

Relationship Type	Time to Partnership Creation
Licensing	1.5 – 3.0 months
Distribution	1.5 – 2.0 months
Marketing	30 – 45 days
Investment	3 – 4 months
Joint development	4 – 6 months
Field sales	2 months

Step 1: Setting Partner Objectives

Partnership objectives should always be tangible, measurable, and associated with a time frame. Loosely defined objectives or those that could be subjective rather than objective will put the alliance manager or group at risk of failure.

As partnership objectives are associated with the corporate objectives, the first step is to attain the list of your company's corporate objectives. If this is not available, attempt to identify the quarterly objectives. In the case of Sunstream Corporation, the two-person management team of Ken Hey and his wife Deborah never had enough time to even think about corporate objectives. Between manufacturing the prototype boat lift, the first boat show, and fulfilling the overwhelming orders, they were always too busy to focus on formal partnerships. After getting more than 40 orders on the first day of the boat show, they just knew that their manufacturing capacity was outstripped eightfold. "We knew we were in trouble when we started asking each other what we would do if we sold more around noontime," Hey explained. "We had no time to think about something as far off as corporate objectives. But we knew we would need them as soon as that first show closed."

They suddenly realized they required a manufacturing partner, and fast. It took them "roughly 15 minutes" to agree on the objectives of the first partnership in company history.

"First we started analyzing our options, and we realized that the biggest challenge was making a good first impression for a new product. We couldn't falter on delivery schedule or quality. However, when we talked with all the shops in town, they couldn't even look at jobs for two months." Hey figured the long turn around time would kill the orders before the checks cleared.

At this point, the corporate objectives created themselves. Consistent quality was the most important. Second was recognizing a partner with the right expertise and a commitment to manufacturing to specification. As Hey realized that the manufacturing was outside Sunstream's financial capabilities, it became imperative that corporate goal number 3 focused on limiting overhead. But when it became apparent that the up-front costs to the manufacturing partner would be in the hundreds of thousands of dollars, Hey had to be willing to sign a long-term partnership agreement. This required a long-term vision and road map. Armed with both, he could comfortably engage in a manufacturing partnership.

Don't Forget the Partners' Objectives

Once you are finished identifying what you need out of a partnership, you need to understand what benefits the partner will realize. In the case of Sunstream, Ken Hey was approached by Chris Michaelson of Elliott Bay Manufacturing, a young boat manufacturing corporation, who had seen the Sunstream booth at the first boat show. Michaelson's corporate goals included leveraging boat and manufacturing experience with his ability to actually finance and manufacture a product. It was a perfect match. Hey needed someone to manufacture, and Michaelson was looking to build something he could understand while continuing to finance and control his own business.

Step 2: Identifying Potential Partners

The planning process truly kicks into gear when you can create a target list of potential partners. The nature of this task requires more than just pulling "the most trafficked Web sites on the net," which the CEO of a large gaming company did to identify potential candidates. It requires an evaluation of your business objectives, needs, and areas of expertise.

When Wormenhoven's team at Network Appliance was forming its initial partnership model, they structured it into three general classes of partnerships. Today the billion-dollar company has five categories, with many subcategories. If you are a small organization like The

Finest Accessories, you might have two categories of partners, or like Front Porch Classics, only one type of partner.

Whether you are large or small, the list of potential partners might initially be very large. Don't worry about the length of the list yet. Just make sure you capture the entire list that is relevant with the category defined.

Assigning Partner Qualifications

Most individuals can think of dozens of potential partners for their business. Ran Slaten of Slaten Painting looked around, saw the Home Depot down the block from his office, confirmed that it had a paint section, and called it a day. Slaten didn't require a process to qualify the opportunity to create a marketing relationship. No other home supply centers that could create a marketing partnership were within two hours of his Quincy, California, business. Others like Sunstream are going to go a step further in their qualification—not because they necessarily want to but because the opportunity and money at stake is so high they can't afford not to.

Determining Relative Values and Using a Potential Partner Scorecard

The first exercise is to identify the most important attributes of a potential partner. Each attribute has a value to your organization, and this is usually a monetary value. Yet values aren't equal in importance throughout your company. As such, the values are relative to one another, and each will have an impact on the corporate objectives. This exercise entails soliciting and confirming the relative values against which each potential partner's organization will be later measured (Table 5–2).

The first step after identifying the most important attributes of a firm is to isolate how the impact on your firm will be measured. For example, a 35-person application software provider ranked the speed of partnership implementation as the most important attribute of a partner. Further identifying the time frame for creation of a partnership eliminates any potential partner with a track record of taking longer than 12 months to create and implement a partnership. This qualification is reviewed along with the ability of the partner to make an investment (number 2), provide technical resources (number 3), and fund the company with joint marketing (number 6).

Table 5–2 Relative Value Worksheet

1. Speed		2. Equity Investment		3. Technology Resources	
Months	Ranking	Yes/No	Ranking	Yes/No	Ranking
0 – 3	10	1,000,000	10	Dedicated architect	10
3 – 6	7	500,000	7	Engineer access	5
6 – 12	5	250,000	5	Developer resource	3
12 +	0	Neither	0	Nothing	0

4. Sales Resources		5. System Integration		6. Comarketing	
People	Ranking	Yes/No	Ranking	Dollars, Thousands	Ranking
15 +	10	Integrators	3	$100 +	10
10	6	License	7	$25 – $100	7
1 – 5	3	OEM/bundling	10	Less than $25	5

7. Sales Channels		8. Noncompetition		13. CAGR	
Industry	Ranking	Industry	Ranking	Rate, Percentage	Ranking
Finance, insurance, and health care	10	Finance, insurance, and health care	10	20 +	10
Finance, insurance	7	Finance, insurance	7	10 – 20	7
Finance	5	Finance	5	Less than 10	4
Government	0	Government	3	Negative	0

9. Market Share		11. Service		12. Potential Licenses	
Precent Ownership	Ranking	Capabilities	Ranking	Units	Ranking
10 – 15	10	Technical	10	1500 +	10
5 – 10	6	Maintenance	7	500 – 1,499	7
Under 5	4	None	5	499 – 0	3

The participants in the relative value session came to agreement on the attribute, its specific deliverables, and its impact on the company. This last aspect was accomplished by assigning a number to the relative importance. Using a scale of 1 to 10, 10 being the highest, each macro attribute received a score.

Using the first attribute, speed of partnership implementation, the three possible partners were assigned a number according to the value placed by the management team. In this case, the shortest time to market received the highest rank of 10.

A slight twist on this example is the ability to deliver revenue in less than 12 months. If each potential partner can deliver revenue, then the attribute requires a weighted relative value separated into amounts: less than $50,000, less than $100,000, and so on.

If you have more than one partner category, expect that the attributes most important to your firm will be different for each category. Once the relative values worksheet is completed for each partner category, use it as the basis for analyzing each potential partner. This creates a scorecard of potential partners (Table 5–3).

Once a scorecard is created for the entire list of potential partners in each category, the final numbers for each attribute are placed on one master sheet. This partner scorecard allows you to review the potential partners, the attributes most important to your firm, confirm if the information used as data was subjective (that is, internal knowledge or common sense as opposed to founded in a historical data point) and the top-line definition of the attribute. By adding the scores, the highest-

Table 5–3 Relative Values Scorecard

Criteria	Objective/ Subjective	Definition	Candidate								
			Hardware			Software			Infrastructure		
			1	2	3	1	2	3	1	2	3
1. Speed	Subjective	Speed of implementation of relationship	10	10	6	6	6	6	10	10	6
2. Equity investment	Subjective	Place an investment	10	7	0	0	7	10	10	10	5
3. Technology resources	Objective	Provide technology and advance notification of SW knowledge to enhance product	10	5	5	3	3	3	3	3	0
4. Sales resource contribution	Subjective	Partner provides people for engineering support	10	3	3	6	6	6	10	6	6
Total score			(40)	25	14	15	22	(25)	(33)	29	17

scoring organizations are isolated, and the process moves to the next partnership planning exercise.

Gain Consensus During Planning

The intent of the relative value exercise is to identify and differentiate potential partners, as well as to gain consensus from your internal management team members. With the decision makers' direct input and participation, downstream alliance creation activities, budgets, and resources are supported much more easily and enthusiastically.

This exercise will take an hour or more depending on the number of candidates, the number of values, and the depth of the discussion that takes place as the individuals come to agreement. Don't rush this process. In and of itself the discussion will be invaluable since you will get to hear prejudices, opinions, fears, and possibly even great ideas come to the forefront.

You will also have the unique opportunity to witness disagreements and conflict among decision makers. Understanding how management conflicts are resolved (even if this includes you) is as important as learning more about the biggest champions and detractors of partnerships. Since this will be accomplished at the beginning of the alliance effort, you will be able to anticipate a whole host of issues that might surface during the partnership development activities.

When The Nature Conservancy (TNC) looked at different potential partners and conducted the relative values exercise, Steve Volkers found that the relative values were colored by TNC employees' own industry initiatives. "We went through an exhaustive evaluation process with multiple potential partners, then narrowed it down to a few," he described. Volkers then applied his own attributes that met with other industry, geographic, and environmental initiatives. Going through the process opened everyone's eyes to the specific needs and issues surrounding particular partners. It also identified prejudices and opinions well before the partner development work actually began.

Step 3: Evaluating Risks to Narrow the Partnership Field Further

Once the most positive aspects of a potential partner are identified, you need to consider the uglier aspects of dealing with an organization. The

Table 5–4 Relative Risks Worksheet

1. Stealing	
Product/Intelligence	Ranking
Very likely	0
Don't know	5
Not likely	10

2. Other Relationships	
Nondisclosure	Ranking
Competitors	3
Noncompetitors	10

3. Staffing Requirements	
Number	Ranking
3 people	10
2 people	5
1 person	0

4. Quality	
Benchmark	Ranking
Very likely	0
Don't know	5
Not likely	10

5. Product Ready	
Ship on time	Ranking
Very likely	0
Don't know	5
Not likely	10

6. Product Performance	
Projected	Ranking
Above expectations	0
As expected	5
Poorly	10

7. Overcapacity	
Extend Resources	Ranking
Very likely	10
Don't know	5
Not likely	0

8. Complexity of Organization	
Time Investment	Ranking
Development	10
Marketing and sales	5
Administration	2

9. Industry Overlap	
Health Care	Ranking
Very likely	10
Don't know	5
Not likely	0

intent behind this evaluation is to raise the partner traits considered the most detrimental to your company. It is also a precursor to understanding your risk management options in the event the worst-case scenario occurs.

The relative risks worksheet follows the exact same process as its values counterpart (Table 5–4). A few of the more common risks identified include infringement on intellectual property or technology, or worse, the transfer of confidential information to other partners. Sales or marketing can mitigate risks by requiring an exclusive deal, an investment, or other restrictive and controlling term.

Once completed, the top three potential partners from the relative values scorecard are evaluated using the relative risks worksheet. Apply the same scoring process to risks as you did to benefits, and you will get a clear picture of which company holds the greatest and the least risk among the partnership candidates (Table 5–5).

The Nature Conservancy is concerned about how potential partnerships will be viewed by the stakeholders; in other words, they need to protect their reputation. "We wouldn't want to brand a gasoline with The Nature Conservancy logo, but it's OK to have them say broadly that they are a supporter," says Volker.

To mitigate the risks of a PPO requesting to participate in the wrong type of campaign, TNC fully explores the entire partnership model during the relative value and risk attributes discussion. They evaluate a combination of customers and suppliers and determine who could meet TNC goals as "good corporate citizens."

Another risk TNC faces is that it might be leaving other PPOs on the table. While it is creating partnerships in what it considers the "smartest manner," it can't possibly reach every organization that could be a good long-term partner. At some point, Volker's team will have to recognize that some of these organizations will partner with another nonprofit group. For that reason, the value assigned is not as high as the first set of risk attributes.

Table 5–5 Relative Risks Scorecard

Criteria	Objective/ Subjective	Definition	Candidate								
			Hardware			Software			Infrastructure		
			1	2	3	1	2	3	1	2	3
1. Potential for stealing product/ intelligence	Subjective	Are they going to reverse engineer for the purpose of stealing our product or intelligence?	5	0	5	5	5	0	0	5	5
2. Other relationships	Subjective	Will they transfer information to other partners?	0	0	5	5	5	5	0	5	5
3. Staffing requirements	Objective	How many full time people does this partnership require for support?	10	3	3	3	3	0	3	3	3
4. Quality benchmark	Objective	Are public benchmarks available?	10	0	0	0	0	0	5	5	0
Total score			25	(3)	13	13	13	(5)	(8)	18	13

Step 4: Determining Partnership Revenue

Another important step in creating a partnership plan is to identify the projected revenue and expense from each potential partner. Granted, some long-term strategic partners are nearly impossible to measure according to experienced managers like Kris Hagerman of VERITAS Software. But the vast majority of small- and medium-size companies are going to be focused on revenue producing, cost-saving partnerships. For this reason, estimated costs associated with the relationship are subtracted from the revenue figures.

After completing the relative risks scorecard, your list of potential partnership candidates should be reduced to a manageable number of three to five organizations. For the financial exercise, it's worthwhile to assess as many firms as can be reasonably evaluated in a short period of time. Sometimes the candidate with the most risk can deliver the highest returns. Understanding the nature of a potential partnership and gaining consensus on either pursuing or declining the opportunity cannot be undervalued. In addition to keeping your course aligned with corporate objectives, future distractions can be refuted based on sound decisions made without internal or external pressures.

Start by identifying the revenue associated with the partnership (Table 5–6). The software firm in this example used publicly available data to estimate the number of customers for each partner and the estimated number of desktop seats using the partner software. It then estimated a modest penetration of that customer base per year.

At a wholesale price of $20,000, the revenue projected through to the partner's own customer base is significant. Additionally, each partner has a distribution channel in place. The software firm did not take the time to assess the partner's channel, the potential sell-through capacity, or associated revenue. Just from completing this initial portion of the financial return, a secondary evaluation of the channel-derived revenue was not required to move forward.

The last part of this equation is to identify the internal and external costs of supporting the relationship. Internally, you might have a part-time or dedicated alliance, technical, or marketing managers. Externally, costs might include a public relations, advertising, or events firm with an associated budget. Discretionary dollars might be required by anticipated partnership-related programs. Behind each line item are

Table 5-6 Partnership Financial Scorecard

	Competitors		
	Hardware	Software	Infrastructure
Projected Revenue			
Users (licenses, visitors)	149,335	123,700	0
Percent share year 1	5%	5%	5%
Price per item	$20,000	$20,000	$20,000
Total projected revenue	$7,466,750	$6,185,000	$0
Projected Costs			
Up-front personnel	1	1	1
Ongoing personnel	2	2	0
Total resource cost	$150,000	$150,000	$0
Outside costs (agencies, consultants)	$0	$0	$0
Total cost	$150,000	$150,000	$0
Total return	$7,316,750	$6,035,000	$0
Cost per lead	$1	$1	$0
Revenue per lead	$49.00	$48.79	$0.00

assumptions of salary and overhead. These figures must be identified and validated in order to be a true assessment of costs.

Ultimately, you are interested in the cost of acquiring a new customer through the partnership. By completing this spreadsheet, you quantify the value a potential partner will have on your organization. Depending on the type of partnership, capital and human resource savings associated with innovation, research and development, sales, support, and marketing can be identified. These numbers are invaluable when you talk to your board or investors.

Step 5: Measuring Partnership Results

The phrase "return on partnership investment" may sound like an oxymoron. Yet fewer than 5 percent of the firms BMG has surveyed has a means to measure its partner relationships. Without clearly defining what success means, gaining agreement as to when you have achieved your goals is open to interpretation. For instance, the goal of "improving customer support" is vague. However, a 10 percent decrease in call volume in the first six months of the year through partnership support is easy to measure and confirm.

The Nature Conservancy's goals for its philanthropic and ECO partnerships were easy to measure—it came down to meeting dollar objectives. Measuring the branding partners, on the other hand, took some creativity. In the end the only way to measure brand awareness was by the number of campaigns delivered, whether or not the campaigns delivered the messages previously identified to the partners, and if the results of increased support met objectives.

For instance, one current marketing campaign TNC is running focuses on saving "the last great places." Partners involved in this campaign contribute dollars to the marketing programs specifically designed around this campaign. General Motors gave money to this campaign, while Microsoft donated in terms of free software for the campaign. Business development vice president Steve Volkers explained, "Our sponsors know money goes toward our efforts in that area. Our deliverable to them is the measured results." In this case, results were measured in how many programs were accomplished, the extent of the reach, and other outcomes by adding new sponsors which would ensure that the goals of the Nature Conservancy are reached.

But Volkers also has the ability to quantify this information, which is not common in partnership development. "We provided all the contributors with an accounting of where their money went." As a former Microsoft executive, Volkers knows how very few partners provide measured information, and fewer still in the nonprofit world provide measured results. Every penny counts for the large nonprofit. The end result is that the partners felt that quantifying the goals reflected the professionalism of TNC as an organization. "Our contributions go for a direct purpose, and our partners know this each time we provide a program review sheet at the end of each calendar quarter."

Choosing the Quantifier

When determining how and if a partnership goal can be measured, be sure to look at the means available to measure the outcome. Revenue sounds easy to measure, but if your internal accounting system doesn't capture the flow-through of revenues by partnerships, arriving at this measurement could be a huge challenge. Informal studies we've conducted show that a majority of small businesses don't invest in these tracking programs, or they are simply too overwhelmed to follow up on this type of data. Thus, only the most generalized information is available.

To start, consider if you would like the information available and who will compile and report this data. Figure out how often you want the information: in real time or batched, as in once a day, once a week, once a month, once a quarter, and so on. This will at least frame the task, assuming you have a support person that can gather the information. And if you aren't the person responsible for attaining this information, determine the right individual(s).

Many large organizations do not like to measure alliances because they are not set up to measure alliances. Many decision makers also believe time spent on measuring an alliance is more costly than the reward. As a former general manager at Microsoft running several billion dollars' worth of NT operating system business, Frank Artale, recounts encouraging the cancellation of a partner contract because "$200,000 wasn't worth the time it took us to figure out if the monies involved each quarter, and send them the invoice, scrap over the dollars, and get the check in." Artale wanted partners that were thinking strategically, building new markets, and working with him for the multiyear, multi-million-dollar payback. "In the end, a hundred or two hundred thousand means nothing if it costs you market leadership." In the final analysis, make sure the intent of the partnership goal matches the partner and cost of the measurement.

Five Steps on Five Slides

With a logical process, paired with models that are simple and easy to understand and employ, your partnership planning outcomes will fit on five pages of a presentation, or in our *PowerPoint* world, five slides. This conveys more than enough information for most senior managers to make a decision about a partnership plan. According to Dan Wormenhoven, even five pages is sometimes overkill. "I want to see three slides. The first with the strategy, the second with the return, and the third with dependencies, risks, and options." The other information is always good as a backup to identify how conclusions were derived.

Accordingly, the five slides are used and reused depending on the needs of the business. Banks and other financial institutions are interested in product development, inventory, and capital expenses, but they are also keen to understand overall market strategies. You should be able to cull this information from your plan. Perhaps the most important reuse of this planning information is when you elect to share your partnership strategy with an existing or potential partner. This sharing of information occurs when a long-term partnership is being discussed and the intended partner desires to understand how it might play a larger role in the growth of your company. It is also requested when a potential partner desires to invest in your firm and must verify competitive issues with future partners.

Partnership Development Life Cycle

CHAPTER HIGHLIGHTS

- *Partnership development three-phase process*
- *Milestones that make or break movement to the next phase*
- *Getting to Wow*
- *Understanding the subtext during the initial partnership development meetings*

A GENERAL NEVER GOES INTO BATTLE without a strategy and plan of execution. During times of war, the best plans are successful only if the action of the fighting troops can be anticipated and managed with choreographed precision.

So it is with all successful partnership development organizations. A capitalist never delivers a product to a market that cannot be manufactured on a sustainable basis. More important, the daily activities of the corporation need to be managed with a military logic, leaving little room for error within the ranks of middle managers.

You now have a partnership development plan that contains the logic behind your corporate and partnership strategies. It also serves as the road map to aiding your partnership development efforts. Now is the time at which you act as the *comitatenses* foot soldiers of Rome past. As the force responsible for penetrating the target organization, you need to understand that the most constant part of partnership development is its cycle, which holds true no matter what industry you are working in, what product you are pitching, or what economic environment exists around you.

Partnership Milestones

Just as the capitalist and military victors are identified by gaining markets and winning hills, the partnership development cycle is presented in terms of milestones achieved, making it easy for your management team to understand the activities directly related to the process. For that reason, the partnership development process is separated into three phases. Each phase includes a *milestone* that must be completed in order to move to the next phase. Within each phase are *interim* milestones leading up to the completion of the *phase milestone.*

Besides absorbing the basic process, you will learn how to intuit the status and progress of the relationship. Through language translation skills, you will be able to decipher what the PPO decision maker is saying to you about your relationship, even if he or she does not offer a direct statement. You will also learn techniques for compressing the time between milestones. This is accomplished by leveraging business, economic, product, or marketing pressure points of the PPO. After reading this chapter, you will be able to customize the standard partnership development life cycle to fit your own needs. This cycle becomes the project plan from which you can easily manage all the related partnership development activities throughout your organization.

Once the partnership strategy and planning activities have been concluded, the partnership development activities begin. The development activities end when the partnership agreement is signed and the transition to ongoing management of the partnership has occurred. In short, partnership development takes place between the planning and the management of the partnership (Figure 6–1).

During the first phase, the financial and personnel requirements are minimal. The primary objective is to attain agreement from the PPO on the business case behind a partnership. Once this has been achieved, phase 2 formally commences. Confirming the validity of the products involved in the partnership is the primary goal of the due-diligence

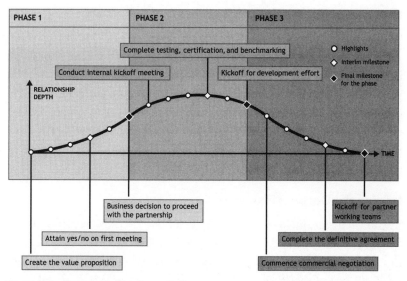

Figure 6–1 Partnership Development Process

phase. Upon completion of the due-diligence phase, an agreement will be created legally binding the two companies. Once this is done, sales and marketing activities will begin.

Phase I

The goal of phase 1 is to validate that an opportunity exists with a potential partner, gain agreement on that point with the potential partner, and evidence this agreement by defining a path to reach the actual partnership (Figure 6–2).

The milestones of phase 1 include a validation call with the potential decision maker, an interim validation point with the confirmed decision maker(s) wherein the high-level pitch is made, and finally the meeting that determines the go/no-go decision to move forward.

The possible outcomes of phase 1 include a verbal agreement by both parties on the business objectives for the partnership. This provides a clear path for progression to the next steps covering the due-diligence process. If this does not occur, then the business case is weak, and the strategic imperatives don't exist.

Creating and Delivering the Business Case

Creating the business case that conveys your proposition for creating value for the potential partner is necessary before the first phone call is ever made. It identifies who you are, why you believe a partnership is worth a discussion, how you propose proceeding, and any time-sensitive considerations. The first pitch of your value proposition must be focused, clean, and on target. Chapter 9 covers oral and written versions of value proposition pitches that serve as guideposts throughout the course of all three partner development phases.

Finding the Decision Maker

Spend whatever time is necessary to ferret out the right decision maker, because time spent at this point will save months of wasted energy and thousands of dollars later on. Many options are available to you either in direct or indirect forms to help you identify the PPO's actual decision maker.

Once a person is identified, the pitch must be delivered, after which the role of the decision maker is then validated. This can be accom-

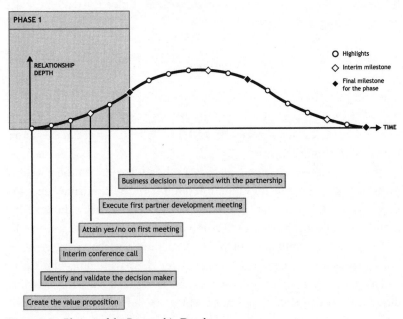

Figure 6–2 Phase 1 of the Partnership Development

plished in less than 30 seconds. The key is to *give* what that person needs, *get* what *you* need, and get off the phone. What you need is a confirmation that you have an interesting partnership opportunity, which could include a commitment to review the value proposition (even if you have already sent it), and a promise for a follow-up conversation to determine the next steps.

Assuming you receive a positive response to your verbal value proposition, you must verify or validate the role and responsibility of your contact. Five questions should always be asked during the verification process. Unless you get a yes to all five of the following questions, ask the person you are speaking to for the recommendation of another person who may be better able to handle your potential partnership. The questions are as follows:

- Are you responsible for setting the strategic agenda for the product and/or market in question?
- Do you have profit-and-loss (P&L) responsibility for the product and/or market in question?
- Do you have strategic imperatives for the next product relevant to my product and market area?
- Are you responsible for selecting, promoting, recommending, and funding partners?
- Can you tell me about a time when you have served as a sponsor for a strategic partnership?

Preventing Wasted Effort

Too many alliance managers believe that everything has to be done in person. This is not smart business. Eliminate your own risk of a mistake by accomplishing as much over the phone as possible. Your guiding philosophy of partnership development should include not wasting a single minute until you have proven a valid partner opportunity exists and the PPO agrees. Your peers and boss will appreciate this cost-saving measure.

During an interim telephone call, first reconfirm that the person you are working with is, in fact, able to drive the intended alliance through the organization. This can save literally months of wasted effort. Second, by giving your contact a business case that is more in-depth, he or she is automatically being set up as an internal champion. Suddenly, your contact is giving you feedback on your deck, poking holes in weak spots, and asking questions that can be addressed before getting into a bigger forum. Third, it enables your contact at the PPO to have a higher degree of confidence in the potential partnership. He or she will fight harder for your case and ensure that the right individuals attend the final phase 1 business development meeting. This commonly eliminates the need for a secondary business meeting (which again, reduces time and money).

During the phase 1 face-to-face meeting, you are likely to hear a number of phrases integral to the success or failure of a relationship. Unfortunately, the meaning of these words and phrases is so expertly camouflaged that it takes an interpreter to know what is really being said. Were everyone to know what to listen for, the path to a successful partnership would be like a wide steel bridge for all to walk, rather than a winding invisible path through the undergrowth.

What Is Said versus What Is Meant

Over my years of working with organizations to create relationships, I have kept a log of what was said and when it was said, and I then followed up with the individuals later to find out what they really meant. Early on, I noticed that the sayings were universal from organization to organization and that they were used in conjunction with the stage of the partnership development activities as opposed to a product in particular. Mostly, I noticed that timing—the actual moment that something was said—is of particular importance.

Understanding the meaning of the few phrases I have noted in Table 6–1 is instrumental in knowing where you really stand with an organization during the first phase of the meeting.

Meeting Closure

Before ending the meeting, ask your primary contact within the PPO if the meeting accomplished the objectives laid forth and if it has stimulated a discussion about the next set of activities. If the objectives were met, the remaining time is spent identifying next steps, owners, time frames, dependencies, and projected costs. If the meeting failed to meet the objectives of one or both parties, the issues are raised to the surface, and a determination is made as to lowering the barriers.

Table 6–1   What Was Said and What Was Meant

What They Said	What They Meant
Your product is compelling.	Interesting product, but it has a ways to go before it meets our needs.
Our products needs to be closer aligned.	We aren't going to work together until you make some changes that use more of our own products first.
Companies that exploit our technology will be in a better position to partner.	Other firms (or products) are in a better position to partner with us based on how they use our product today.
The product teams need to have a technical due-diligence process meeting.	We'd like to see if your product works as well as you say it does.
We work on an aggressive schedule.	You've got a window of opportunity, and if you want to meet it, you've got to seriously adjust your timeline.
How much intellectual property do you have?	We might consider an investment or acquisition, and need to know if the product can be protected by patents or trademarks.
How much money are you prepared to spend on partner activities with us?	Partnering with you may not be associated with product or technical development. It might just be positioning. If that's the case, it all comes down to the number of bucks that can be spent. The more money, the stronger the relationship.
What is your partnership model?	Are you working with our competition, and if so, how do you plan on differentiating our products? Are we going to be favored in your model?
Who knows of your intentions?	Do you have an executive sponsor within your organization aware of this, and can he or she support the decisions?
What is your valuation?	You might be an interesting acquisition candidate, and it's good to know if you fit within our budget.

Accelerators for Phase 1

The average duration of phase 1 is three months. If you are aggressively managing the partnership development cycle, allocate two weeks to identifying and validating the right decision maker within your target partner's organization. The next two weeks should be set aside for their receipt and review of your value proposition as well as the first phone call. An interim call between the two organizations might take another two weeks, and the first in-person meeting another two weeks. This cuts out 30 days from the basic cycle.

A few things can be done to reduce the time frame even further. It starts with targeting the right company, of course, and having a well-thought-out business proposition. Here are a few specifics:

1. Get an agreement from your CEO on what the press release will read. This press release, which in theory is what you would send to the press after the partnership is formed, is shorthand for setting the foundation for the value proposition and intent behind the vision of the partnership. This guiding light should govern all future activities.
2. Use current events to create time imperatives and incentives for the potential partner. Use these to your advantage every time you leave voice or e-mail messages.
3. Try to identify another potential partner for the PPO to pursue that would not be competitive to your own company. This shows you are thinking about what is good for the PPO's product line and spending the extra time and energy. This also puts the PPO in your debt, and its management might feel compelled to actually read your value proposition or set up a meeting.
4. Create the value proposition during the development of the partnership plan.

Phase 2

Once you have accomplished the objective of a go decision for the partnership, you seamlessly transition into the next phase. This part of the cycle is called *product due-diligence review* (Figure 6–3). The due-diligence review is as benign as test driving a car. Before you buy, you want to try. In return, you expect two things. First, the car will be fully functional, and second, the car dealer will run a credit check on you before giving a loan. This is a bidirectional due-diligence process that most individuals encounter many times throughout their life. When it comes to a business application, the process may take more time, but it is usually less intrusive than a complete financial disclosure.

The goal of phase 2 is to validate that the product(s) work as stated. This evaluation is made in order to understand how the products used within the partnership will work together.

The milestones of phase 2 include the initial meeting between the technical teams and internal certification. The tangible outcome is a product-level plan that serves as the basis for a partner agreement.

Phase 2 can be accelerated by leveraging product development schedules, new market opportunities, or resource availability by either team. It can also be accelerated if product certification or result-oriented benchmarking is performed before the technical discussions take place.

The Phase 2 Process

The second stage of partnership development starts at the point when both firms have agreed to the business opportunity. This occurs either at or shortly after the phase 1 meeting. If it happens sooner, then the PPO is very excited about the partnership. Now is the time to verify that what has been presented can in fact be accomplished.

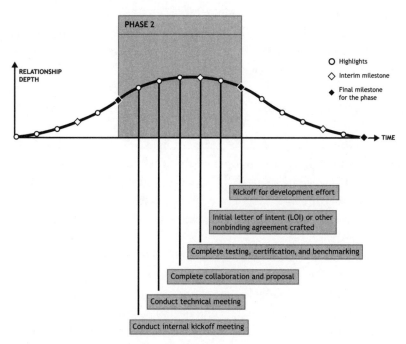

Figure 6–3 Phase 2 of the Partnership Development

A virtual hand-off is made from the business team to those responsible for reviewing the product. Once done, an opinion will be offered to the business team that is more like a verdict. It will be taken as final.

Small, unproven firms or new business units share the common challenge of proving that their product works. The larger firm typically employs its resources to determine if its own credibility will be damaged in any way through a relationship with your company. Sometimes this phase gets so jumbled it can take from 6 to 12 months, but a well-orchestrated effort can accomplish the same result in a time frame of 1 to 3 months.

Matching the Intent with the Process during the Due-Diligence Process

The intent behind understanding the potential partner's product strengths and weaknesses requires both companies to reveal proprietary product details. As such, it's important to limit the scope of the due-diligence evaluation as well as the number of individuals included at each level. This contains the risk of unwanted information getting into the hands of the wrong people.

The way to effect control is to create the process with your alliance manager peer at the PPO. You will want to identify the objective—what needs to be seen, by whom, and when—as well as the intent behind the objective. For instance, an objective of the PPO might be to determine how easy it is to use a product. On the surface, you might interpret this to mean how fast a consumer can make the product operational. However, your potential partner might not care at all how "fast" a consumer can learn how to operate the machine. Instead, the PPO is concerned about time spent in the service, support, and maintenance of the product. In reality, the PPO is going to stress-test the product to see how much it breaks, how often, and what risk it might incur from the customer.

One example of this type of subversive due-diligence procedure occurred with Sunstream Corporation. Early on, potential partner Cobalt was concerned about how long it would take to train the boat owners to use the new boat-launching technique. Cobalt's dealers voiced anxiety that instead of being an "add-on" sale to the boat, the need for a special lift would create the perception that Cobalt boats were hard to manage, which would discourage customers from purchasing them.

During the initial partnership efforts, Cobalt dealers were stunned to realize that consumers were using their boats three to four times as much as other boat owners. Once trained to use the boat lift, it was much easier to raise and lower the boat into the water. This made the overall "experience much more satisfying," according to Ken Hey, Sunstream's CEO.

In turn, Cobalt dealers reported two significant results that directly impacted revenue. First, consumers who used the boat lifts were trading up boats every 15 months as opposed to the 48 months for boat owners without the Sunstream lift. Second, these same consumers were so enthusiastic about their boat lifts that it became the single repeated reason that their friends and families purchased a Cobalt boat. Hey began receiving reports from Cobalt dealers who said existing Cobalt boat owners would come into the showroom with friends, point out the boat lift, and then describe the boat. The "ease-of-use approach was the deciding factor for the consumers."

Had Hey not identified the real issue behind Cobalt's due-diligence process, he would not have been able to accurately address the true concern in such a beneficial manner.

The Technical Due-Diligence Process Matrix

One of the ways to ensure that the intent of the due-diligence evaluation matches the process and outcome is to identify with your potential partner the aspects of the product and company to be reviewed during the due-diligence effort itself. If you haven't been through this process before, it will be comforting to know that only a modest number of items need to be reviewed for the majority of alliances created (Table 6–2).

Utilize this matrix as a baseline of activities that might be requested during the due-diligence phase. Seek to understand the intent behind a request that does not match up with the matrix before putting on your protective armor. The potential partner might have a very good reason for requesting something out of the ordinary, such as an investment in your firm. Yet this might depend upon a single detail of the product not commonly associated with one type of agreement.

This has happened in situations in which a partnership started as a primarily sales and marketing relationship but evolved during the due-diligence portion to become more intriguing to the product development group. This led to internal discussions within the PPO about a minority investment. The lead product manager at the PPO asked to

Table 6–2   Technical Due-Diligence Evaluation

	Marketing	Licensing	OEM	Joint Development
Certification	X	X	X	X
Remote testing		Sometimes	X	X
On-site set-up and testing			X	X
Customer service and support testing			X	X
Spot check of technology			X	X
Testing reviews				X
Documentation review				X
Process review			Sometimes	X
Customer interview				X
Reseller or channel interview			X	X

test a particular product and see relevant documentation without divulging the reason. This request was taken as a competitive threat instead of the opportunity for a deep relationship. Ultimately, the product manager was so focused on getting a look at the product, he showed his hand regarding an investment.

Wisely, the smaller firm was glad to provide the product information, but only after a letter of intent was signed, stating an investment would be completed if the objectives of the product review were met. To the satisfaction of both parties, the product review did meet the requirements of the product manager, an investment was placed, and the partnership was immediately elevated to a strategic partnership for both organizations.

Hands-On Management to Protect Your Firm

Now is the time to have a meeting with the technicians within your organization who will support the effort. This discussion also provides to other organizations within your firm who are critical to the success of the partnership a recap of partnership development activities to date. Not necessary prior to this point, these people are now responsible for fashioning the strategic cornerstone of the partnership.

To ensure that everyone is onboard with the strategy, expectations are set as to the processes, time frames, and risks. Individuals in research and development tend to be detail and process oriented. Remember the time constraints faced by the product and development groups, who are usually overburdened with deadlines and other pressures. Don't be surprised if your "exciting opportunity" is initially viewed with dismay. Until you convince the team otherwise, your opportunity will be a whole lot of new work without any visible return.

This feeling will change from skepticism to support as the team melds the business justification with areas of opportunity for the products to work in concert with one another. The best outcome is one wherein the group catches onto the partnership vision and additional partnership opportunities are inspired by creative product-related scenarios.

The technical due-diligence meeting itself is usually held at the site of the larger organization. Doing so allows the host company to invite all the individuals who play the role of a stakeholder in the partnership.

Getting to Wow

During the meeting, products are presented and sometimes used to highlight certain features. Many companies attempt to provide a visual representation of a finished product by presenting a prototype. If the conversation is positive, future partnership what-if situations might be included as well. This last activity is known as a *white-boarding session*. It is the time when the PPO has captured the vision and is brainstorming previously ignored opportunities. Frank Artale refers to this state as "getting to Wow." "Nothing really matters up until the point when the engineering team on the other side of the table gets excited enough to capture the vision," he comments.

When you have made a compelling business proposition that results in a technical discussion, it's vital that the product teams are excited enough to be impressed. If you don't get the team on the other side to say "Wow," then you might have a great business case, but in the long run you haven't impressed the teams that matter. Artale believes all strategic partnerships are based in a relationship where both teams are equally excited, enthusiastic, and inspired to work toward a partnership. "You need to go into the technical meeting with the single objective of getting the other side to sit back in their chairs and say, 'Now that's impressive.'"

This meeting concludes with agreement from both sides to move forward with the product due-diligence evaluation that has not yet occurred. It also includes product feature and functionality issues or requests for minor product changes, potentially from either side. This can be as simple as certification, or verified compliance with the potential partners' solution, or as complex as a complete re-creation of your (or the PPO's) product lines. Most technical due-diligence sessions for strategic relationships have outcomes somewhere in the middle—the product doesn't have to be entirely re-created, but it wasn't a slam-dunk, in-and-out session with no product changes.

Owning the Technical Meeting

Your ability to manage and control the due-diligence process is the number 1 factor in achieving your objectives and reducing the risk along the way.

Conduct the Due-Diligence Review at Your Site   While I've stated before that most due-diligence reviews happen at the larger partner's site, the reasons for wanting it at your place of business are obvious. You will absolutely have more control over the product environment, and you will be able to pull in the individuals who can best represent the product strategy. This affords you the opportunity to establish credibility and articulate a sustainable growth plan with minimal cost to your company. The risks then are also reduced as fewer individuals from the PPO organization are exposed to your product details.

Manage the Meeting and Topics to Be Covered   Even if the meeting is held at the PPO's site, it is reasonable to expect you will manage the meeting, particularly as you are representing the firm instigating the discussions.

Start by preparing the questions that need to be answered by both parties. This raises assumptions and preconceived notions by the other party that directly influence the topics raised. Particular aspects of the product demonstration and discussion are also reviewed internally and with your counterpart. More often than not, your own technical team will request a look into the PPO's product line not publicly available. Chances are slim that future product plans will be covered automatically unless you request these areas be covered by the PPO. Last, managing the meeting means you will know beforehand how far your technical team is willing to compromise or otherwise consider product modifications to achieve your stated objective. Your team needs to be uniform in the support of the objective and the parameters of compromise in order to answer direct questions during the meeting. The ability to do this greatly impacts the ability of the PPO to gain a clear understanding of what it takes to work with your firm.

For example, the product you offer is a new type of in-home heart monitoring device, but the potential partner already offers a widget of sorts, albeit not as good as your own. Are you prepared to give up your own, even if it's not as good, to gain a closer relationship with the organization? If so, what will it cost, how will this impact the customer base, and will the positioning of the product in the marketplace be put at a disadvantage? These are truly strategic questions, and questions that had to be answered by Phillip Benz and the other executive staff members at Advanced Vascular Dynamics. They cannot be answered by the technology lead alone. Sometimes even the board gets involved in these kinds of discussions *prior* to the technical meeting.

The reason is simple. The technical representative will be armed with the knowledge of exactly how far the company is willing to go in consideration of the relationship, and the alliance manager in turn can be prepared to set the stage for negotiation of the appropriate agreement. Unprepared participants at the technical discussions can be very damaging to the overall discussion. For example:

- Lack of creativity will be viewed as narrowmindedness. If you can't think out of the box and provide well-thought-out responses to suggested ideas, your organization is not perceived as visionary.
- Lack of a strategy and plan will come across as disorganized. The preceding chapter identified a five-slide partnership plan. One of these slides conveys your partnership model and strategy. It's important that you be able to articulate your partnership model verbally as well as integrate other potential partners of mutual interest during the discussion. This will present a picture of an organization who can build the bridge connecting strategy with a path of tactical execution.
- Lack of a proposal will come across as ad hoc and random. A good salesperson knows the sales call always ends with a statement to

close the business and progressive steps required to do so. Partnership development is similar. If the meeting has covered the objectives and addressed open issues, the discussion shifts to reaching an agreement on the next steps and the specific deliverables.

Plan for Contingencies   Attending the meeting is entirely different from owning the meeting. Determine which role your organization will play, and strive to make it a reality. The outcome of having everyone on the same page and understanding parameters prior to the point of making a decision will save surprises and usually lots of money.

Several years ago I represented a client in the Internet commerce business. During the first technical meeting, over 20 software engineers showed up for a discussion when we were anticipating 3. It turned out that five groups within the PPO had a vested interest in the partnership my client and the PPO were considering. Of these, two believed they had directly competitive products. It was their mission to stop a relationship at all costs. And yes, they said this directly in the meeting!

Fortunately, we had prepared for a scenario of uninvited and antagonistic participants with overlapping products. Prior to the meeting, I had forced the executive staff to consider each and every challenge that might be presented and to think through an initial, and then a preferred response. Then we created a contingency plan for each major issue.

As each opposing party made a case against moving forward with the partnership, he or she heard how my client's product could integrate and complement the opposing solution. Simply "turning off" certain features nullified at least one point of contention. The result was immediate as four engineers and one business manager from the PPO group suddenly recognized an opportunity to extend their own product line into a new market. By addressing their concerns, the team was converted from antagonists to supporters of the partnership.

Compromising on Product   In another client situation, one product out of five presented during the due-diligence review directly overlapped with the PPO's, competing at all levels. We knew that if the PPO understood this overlap, it would be a deal killer. The options were few: Walk away from what we believed to be a relationship that had the potential to produce several million dollars in revenue within the next 12 months, or walk away from the table based on the principle of better technology.

And yet they didn't. In this situation, my client's executive staff recognized their product was far superior to that of the potential partner. They suspected the partner wouldn't dispute that fact but had spent so much money on marketing efforts that it would be impossible to take the inferior product off the market. So the executive team asked their own product group if using the PPO's product instead of its own would cause customer dissatisfaction or attrition. The answer received from the product group was a negative. At that point, the executive management agreed they would rip their own product and replace it with the PPO's if asked, but not before.

Doing so made a joint development agreement likely as my client asked for, and received, the funding for this activity. In return, the PPO was able to announce that an industry leader (my client) chose their product in favor of its own. This sent a message to the market about the quality of the PPO's product line.

Both firms agreed that a strategic relationship inclusive of sales and marketing support from the PPO was necessary. Our client would definitely require assistance jump-starting sales of existing products to compensate the delayed launch of their new product line.

This logic led the team to assess the financial impact of both the strategic and tactical advantages of the partnership. We were not halfway through the exercise when it became obvious that the client had far more to gain from displacing its own product than fighting for its survival. First it would receive money for the development effort, it would receive marketing support to create awareness and demand, and it would also receive a broader reach than it would have had on its own. The strategy of inserting an inferior product in their product line was a tradeoff, enhancing the other departments within the organization.

It was the value gained by preparing for the technical due-diligence meeting that ensured a successful outcome. The executive management, product, marketing, and engineering team had to weigh the options, the potential upside, and the risk involved in a "rip-and-replace" strategy. This is a lot of effort for a "potential" outcome. Be sure your firm is the one to capitalize on the opportunities afforded by the technical due-diligence phase.

Moving from Discussion to a Tangible Product Proposal

Before a partnership agreement can be created, the product team needs a product plan that addresses the development requirements. This plan is made in a collaborative fashion with the potential partner. This might be a sit-down meeting where both parties brainstorm possibilities, list pros and cons, and then return to their own internal groups for input and consensus. This feedback eliminates the risk associated with partner making while giving the supporting players on your own team a stake in the outcome. If they feel included in the process, they will likely feel obligated to make the outcome a success.

While the internal team reviews the objectives and the potential paths for delivering the necessary changes, you and your product manager set out to unearth the specific costs associated with the effort. By monetizing the cost of the partnership at this early stage, two things happen. First, you become comfortable with attaching dollar values to every effort attributable to the partnership. This is rare in today's environment and a good habit to form. Second, it helps establish your negotiating position of strength or weakness prior to phase 3.

Concurrent or just following this activity is product testing. Depending on the availability of publicly available tests, this can be done ahead of time during phase 1 where it can be used as an accelerator.

In addition to testing and certification, competitive benchmarks might be required. Benchmarking enables the PPO to gauge the performance of your product against its own or other competitive products. In either case, it is in your best interest to understand the benchmark parameters before agreeing to participate. You also want to be involved in the benchmarking activity if you are not allowed to perform the testing and submit the results. Lastly, determine whether the results of the product benchmarking will be shared outside the testing group (that is, with your competition).

As these two efforts wind down, you should be creating the first partnership agreement. This can be either a non-legally binding *letter of intent* (LOI) or a legally binding *memorandum of understanding* (MOU). Either document can be used to emotionally bind the two organizations around the intent of the partnership.

Usually the details of the partnership, such as the product road map, terms and conditions, and associated dollars are not included in this agreement. Instead, the intent of the partnership is supported by setting a conclusive date for completing a formal agreement. With this in place, the beginnings of a trust-based relationship are formed. Each party will start working on the details of the partnership even in the absence of a formal partnership.

Once the agreement is signed, firms are comfortable dedicating resources to a partnership. This will most often be the case when an economic, competitive, or market-driven factor has accelerated the partnership development activities.

Accelerators for Phase 2

One way to speed up the process is by reviewing the testing and certification Web site of the intended partner. Most company Web sites list the requirements for the basic types of partnerships. Determine the cost, the status, and probable outcomes. Doing this will save lots of time up front if it's confirmed that the requirements are too far out of reach for your present state.

Another way to accelerate phase 2 is by anticipating the list of desired features either before or after the first meeting. Expect both parties to offer product improvement suggestions. In the process, be sure to request a ranking of the wish list so it can be prioritized in your own considerations. Be sure that you also understand the logic and intent behind the product change request. This will help you figure out if an easier, less costly way of achieving the same thing can be managed.

Last, use props during the meeting: Specifically, formulate a product proposal design for the audience. The best partnership proposal is a project plan that is necessary when the joint effort requires assistance from the partner organization. The next best partner proposal is a spreadsheet detailing activities and costs. This is more desirable for marketing and distribution agreements. Even if you aren't sure which one to use, preparing and submitting an intelligent document based on the needs of the partnership will put you leagues ahead of the competition.

Phase 3

The goal of phase 3 is to create and complete a formal partnership agreement (Figure 6–4). This is sometimes called a *definitive agreement* because it is considered the final document. The specific type of agreement (distribution, marketing, joint development, and so on) can have many names depending on the actual *type* of relationship and the *components* of the relationship.

The interim milestone for the third phase is the completion of the final agreement. The final milestone is the formal kickoff of the part-

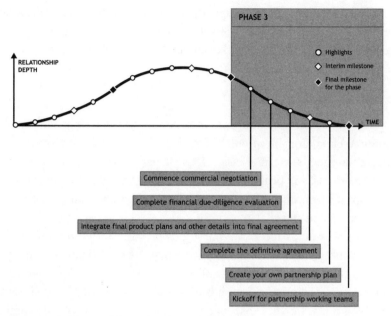

Figure 6–4 Phase 3 of the Partnership Development

nership within both organizations, preceded by the transition of the management of the relationship from the alliance manager to the business development manager.

Accelerators in this phase are based on achieving pricing agreement, which requires that the primary stakeholders including management reach a consensus. Also required is that each organization work with the other organization to ensure a complete understanding of each other's financial parameters. The secondary accelerator is working with the negotiating lead for a seamless transition.

Negotiating the Final Agreement

Depending on the nature of the agreement, negotiation begins in earnest after the initial agreement has been signed. Since the product road map is complete, the negotiating will focus on the price, the timing, payment terms, and conditions, as well as other business practice terms such as penalties and incentives of the partnership.

To achieve a final agreement, an additional due-diligence activity will take place. Instead of the focus being on product health and integrity, it is on the financial standing of your firm.

Unlike banks requesting a common set of information for approval of a loan, corporate entities' requests can range from profit-and-loss statements to a list of assets, customer forecasts, vendor debt, or personal financial statements. The documentation requested depends on the nature of the relationship and the risk perceived by the PPO. The deeper the relationship, the higher the dollars and risk, the more information requested. As a rule of thumb, marketing, sales, and distribution agreements are limited to speaking to customers and vendors. Joint development ventures, investments, and acquisitions demand a very in-depth review of the executive team.

Table 6–3 ties the level of disclosure with general types of partnerships. If information beyond what is listed is being requested, make sure you understand explicitly the reasons for disclosure, and determine on a case-by-case basis if this is absolutely critical to the closure of the partnership deal. Nine times out of ten the information requested is completely irrelevant to the agreement.

The following is a list of items that should never be necessary to close a partner agreement:

Table 6–3 Financial Due-Diligence Analysis Matrix

Appropriate Information to Disclose	Licensing	Distribution	Marketing	Investment or Acquisition
Product revenues	X	X	X	X
Company revenues	X	X		X
Processes, methodologies, services	X	X		X
Resources (personnel)	X	X	X	X
Client list	X		Partial	X
Intellectual property	X			X
Current partner list	X	X	X	X
Status of agreements with all partners	Sometimes	Sometimes	Sometimes	X
Company P&L statement				X
Bank account statements				X
Certified financial audit				X

1. *Individual financial statements* However, it is justified to provide personal financial statements when a joint venture is being considered and the agreement has specific terms around personal liability. It is reasonable to provide this when funding is provided by a third party who desires a guarantee or recourse in case your firm fails to deliver on the product milestone(s). Even so, these requests are rare and should be avoided.
2. *Vision statements for products* Ideas at a conceptual level are fine, but nothing tangible should be handed over that could be taken and delivered to a competitor.

Integrating Product Plans into a Final Agreement

The intent behind incorporating the product plans into the agreement as an appendix is to prevent change in requested product features once the agreement is signed. This single aspect so often overlooked saves each firm from financial exposure and other legal liabilities. It also aids in meeting product delivery schedules on time as a product plan includes a formal completion date. This obligates both parties to specific deliverables. This also ensures the final agreement is concluded by the date identified in the letter of intent.

It is your task to ensure that the written formal document matches the intent of the partnership. Attorneys will be involved to ensure that the language within the agreement supports the intent of the partnership as well as protects your organization. As the alliance manager, you will facilitate and moderate issues between your firm and the PPO's legal team.

Preparing for the Transition

If you haven't already developed a partnership development life cycle timeline, now is the time. You can use either an *Excel* spreadsheet or *Microsoft Project*. For simple projects, an *Excel* spreadsheet will do the job. For years, most of our partner development programs were managed in *Excel* since *Microsoft Project* is not an application most CEOs use on a daily basis. This prepares the relationship manager to coordinate the efforts among the internal and external groups.

When creating your own partnership timeline, include weekly project meetings starting with phase 2. Until the first milestone is met, it's not necessary to consume time from a wider circle of individuals. Yet once the ball is in play, weekly huddles keep the program on track. Also, estimate three internal review cycles for each major deliverable. Be realistic about the time it takes to gain review, have a discussion about the relevant feedback, make changes, and gain final agreement.

Some of this discussion will occur during a partnership kickoff meeting. Attending this meeting will be individuals from each functional department at both organizations. The project plan review is followed by technical or product discussions ensuring that the entire group is up to date on the future and vision of the partnership.

Ongoing program management coordination protocol is established, as is reporting and feedback mechanisms, conflict resolution processes, and an escalation process should executive review be a component of the alliance management.

Accelerators for Phase 3

The most important things you can do to close the deal fast are to know what you want and know what your limits are. Also, if you have been the primary person driving the relationship, try to find someone else to negotiate the deal.

In the middle of phase 2, your product and financial teams should start developing the possible deals to satisfy the intent of the partnership. Set expectations about the pricing, the logic behind the pricing, and buy-in from the management and the board if necessary during this time. Having these parameters in place aids in planting the seeds of pricing with your business peer well before phase 3 comes around. Doing so also aids your peer in setting expectations with the management of the partner organization.

Identify the financial thresholds of the executive team—including the development, marketing, and sales managers and the CEO. In the process, continually set expectations about the terms and conditions.

7

Navigating the Maze

CHAPTER HIGHLIGHTS

- *The four best entry points within a large organization*
- *The best way to reach executives*
- *The fastest route to getting a partnership proposal reviewed*

FOR SEVERAL HUNDRED YEARS, two Roman states—the Greek east and the Roman west—composed the Roman Empire. The outside world made no distinction between east and west. It was one, monolithic, all-powerful organization. Within this structure, functional groups existed, and the leaders of these groups were called *prefects* or *vicars*. Sub-groups abounded, as did entanglements, overlapping roles, and power struggles.

To understand how this organization worked, visualize yourself as the proprietor of a roadside shop, and you believe that an audience with the emperor will propel your new product beyond your neighborhood and out into the rest of the known world. To get the emperor's attention, you have to wind your way through the right diocese and prefectures, skirt the snake pits, step over the dead bodies of past failures, and give a compelling value proposition to the vicars, who might pass along your message to the emperor.

Today, many of the world's leading companies have similar organizational structures. You have to identify the right decision maker, provide the incentive to win support for your case, avoid entities with potential conflict, and ultimately, present your case to a current executive. Failure can and does sometimes result in a fate of business death. On the other hand, success means support, market dominance, and assistance at all levels of the organization.

The Secrets of Organization Charts

Large companies are, by definition, ever changing and dynamic, riddled with false starts and dead ends. Few make their organizational charts public. Entering and navigating the maze of an organization in an effort to create a partnership can and usually does take months. It takes the average business 18 to 24 months between making the first phone call to collecting the first dollar from a partnership. More than half that time is spent simply navigating the maze, or identifying the right person in the right department who makes partnership decisions. When these challenges are resolved, the entire partnership development process is accelerated.

This chapter identifies four of the most common functional departments wherein partner decisions are made. For each group, the purpose, structure, and decision makers are identified. Useful data points are included so you will know what to expect when you engage with the department. Any cost or challenges associated with a particular group are identified as well so you will be well prepared for every situation. After reading this chapter, you will have a far greater understanding and appreciation of your potential partner and what it will take to get to—and through—the initial door.

Situation Profile

Peering into an organization from the outside is difficult. Barriers of all types are erected by organizations seeking to prevent unwanted persons from navigating their maze. Unwanted poachers such as recruiters, competitors, and solicitous vendors are stymied by the lack of a published organizational chart or a phone book or the company's refusal to process requests to speak with someone in a particular position, as opposed to a name. In the struggle to get over, under, and around these barriers, most fail to answer even simple questions and lose confidence prematurely. Here are just a few common causes of frustration in the beginning phase of the partnership development cycle:

- The organization is so big that I don't know where to start.
- When I looked at the Web site of the potential partner organization, I found a half dozen "partnership programs." Some cost money and others don't. I have a small budget and no clue what's going to give me the best return.
- I want a joint development agreement. I don't know if I should speak with the marketing or product development department.
- It's taken me three months to find the right decision maker, and I thought she liked my product. But after three weeks she won't return my calls. What happened?

Industry Averages for First Partnership Development Phase

Over the last six years, my firm has been collecting partnership-related information from every client. This was done to track and measure performance metrics concerning partnership creation. Here are just a few of the discouraging statistics we found as we collected data on companies trying to navigate the maze (Table 7–1).

Often, reality is harsher than averages. Sabre, a provider of travel reservation systems, thinks nothing of a partnership development process that requires *six* face-to-face meetings just to get acquainted. Each meeting takes prospective partners one more step up the ladder toward reaching a partnership agreement.

Laurie Erickson, CEO of The Finest Accessories, recently formed a joint development and manufacturing partnership with cellular phone manufacturer Motorola. Even though Motorola was courting her, the cost of completing the initial steps leading to the deal "exceeded $30,000." How much is the cost, then, for organizations to deal with prospective partners that do not identify a process to help you get what you want? The answer is, Way too much!

Partnership development success is gained through patience, persistence, and resilience. Almost all alliance managers start out with the same disadvantages and advantages. Let's begin with the business of getting to the right place and the right person and then delivering the right value proposition.

Table 7–1 Partnership Development Averages

Activity	Industry Average
Number of phone calls placed until first conversation	22
Number of e-mails sent before first response	9
Number of times the "primary contact" changed before finding the right decision maker	6
Number of hours worked before getting to the first conversation with "final" decision maker	16
Months it took to get the first in-person meeting	2.2
Number of meetings before a yes was given to pursue a partnership	6
Number of different documents used until "go" decision	7
Number of individuals involved from the initiating organization until first meeting	5
Approximate dollars spent in airfare and travel before a "go" decision to pursue initial phase of partnership	$12,500

If your company is like most companies, your budget can't accommodate $30,000 to get a final decision, let alone an initial decision. To spend the least amount of money for the highest return, you need to build upon the AllianceMapping exercise. Having identified the right PPOs, the next steps are the following:

- Map out the organizational structure of the PPO.
- Isolate the primary target groups within the PPO.
- Understand what you can expect when attempting to work with each group.
- Discover how to get around barriers that are put in the way.
- Know when to work groups simultaneously.

Growing Pains

When companies exceed 100 employees, teams are formed to create functional departments. Generally speaking, these departments fall into the categories of product, administration, operations, marketing, sales, finance, and development. As a midsize company extends the number of people it employs, it also builds out the supporting infrastructure, or the tools and processes required in support of the personnel. Over time, a product group is parsed into multiple groups and ultimately may be organized by product divisions. The same holds true for marketing, which may start out as one central organization and then splinter into corporate marketing and product marketing. Over time even this extends to subgroups focused on specific vertical markets, industries, or geographic territories.

Each growth spurt is followed by an associated pain. These are experienced by the individuals within the organization that must do without a formal structure, goal, or sometimes the physical equipment necessary to get the job done. This is compounded by the old Harvard Business School principle that a company fundamentally changes every time it doubles. It changes in terms of departments required, job functions utilized, facilities, operations—literally every aspect of the business. If this is to be believed, then a company is going to double nearly four times between the time it reaches 100 employees and reaching large-company status.

This presents a challenge of tremendous proportions for a prospective alliance manager on the outside desiring to get inside. Consider the job and title shifts involved, the organizational "realignments," even changing phone extensions. This is hard enough for the employees to endure; let alone someone on the outside!

The Four Best Entry Points

The good news is that for all the changes a company will make on its way to becoming a powerhouse, the responsibilities of four of the working groups almost always remain constant. Thus, in companies of around 100 employees, the partnership-related decisions are centralized in four primary functional departments. Fortunately, the use of these working groups aligns well with the goals and intent of partnership development. As these four components are integral to Alliance-Mapping, part of your work has already been completed. Now you can determine which entry point makes the most sense at this time.

The four primary entry points for partnership-related decisions are the following:

1. *The online partner group:* An entirely Web-based portal used to manage the registration and cataloging of prospective partners.
2. *The central partner group:* Staffed by individuals responsible for working directly with a company to create and manage a partnership.
3. *The product group:* Responsible for defining, creating and delivering a product to market. The product group determines the build-versus-buy scenarios—what is to be created internally, purchased externally, or delivered jointly with a partner.
4. *The corporate development group:* Responsible for investing in and acquiring companies or company assets identified by product groups as integral to the long-term goals of the company.

The organizational structure in three of the four groups is consistent. Each group is usually led by a general manager or vice president, and it generally exists at the corporate headquarters. It is important to remember, however, that the larger the organization, the more likely it is that some of the groups you need may be located in the field. Research and development groups, for example, usually sit in the field.

Different industries have unique nomenclature. Product groups in the entertainment and media industries are usually referred to as *content groups.* Corporate development in the finance and insurance industries may be *mergers and acquisitions* (M&A). Business development in the manufacturing industry can really mean sales. Make it a point to know the right terminology in your own industry.

The Online Partner Group

Entry point number 1 is the online partner group. It is the *fastest and cheapest way to establish an entry-level relationship with a PPO.* The online partner group is no more than a Web-based registration form. This serves as a "no-touch" point of entry for all inquiries related to creating a relationship with the PPO. It is called "no-touch" because no one from the PPO gets physically involved in the process. This central point serves as a clearinghouse that filters, files, and distributes communications from a potential partner like letters in a mailroom. These letters are carried electronically to other departments within the company that might be interested in pursuing a relationship.

Approaching the Online Partner Group The PPO's online partner group is important at three times during an outside company's growth from a small to a large business. The first point is when the outside company is just starting *product development* and it needs basic information about the PPO and its products or services. Using the online group accelerates product-oriented activities such as product certification.

The second time is when the outside company is seeking company or product *visibility*. For a young company to have its name posted on the partnership page of a larger company adds credibility and creates initial leads. It can also build awareness of the outside firm throughout the PPO. This is particularly useful to geographically dispersed sales and marketing organizations within the PPO who are looking for a specific partner in a category or region. Syscom Services, a reseller of hardware and software applications specifically tailored for use by professional associations, used its online partner portal to find an appropriate software provider.

Professional associations generally have a central office supported by multiple district offices around the country, which are used to work with members on a local basis. Keeping licenses current requires the association to train and certify all its members, which is an extremely costly endeavor for both the members and the association. Syscom had been looking for a distance-learning tool for several years, but none had proved satisfactory. When its partner portal identified Australian Web-based software provider Southrock Ltd. as a potential partner, Syscom immediately set out to validate the product. Once done, it partnered with Southrock to fill the solution gap in the online learning area, and Southrock became a sales, marketing, and service partner.

The last time to utilize the online partner group is when *the outside organization is ready to create a multifaceted relationship*. Extending the relationship cannot happen if the outside company hasn't completed the fundamental program offerings of the PPO's online partner group. Young companies, tempted by the allure of working "directly" with a product or marketing group, often want to skip the online route. Yet many PPOs consider the online listing a yardstick by which to measure how serious the outside company is about partnering. Using the online partner portal shows that the outside company has taken the time to identify and partic-ipate in the offered programs, taking full advantage of what the PPO has to offer before asking to participate in more programs.

In the last six years, BMG has found that less than 10 percent of firms have taken advantage of the online partner group. This is a shame. Just when a firm decides it's time to pursue a significant part-nership and knocks on the PPO's door, it gets no answer. The sole rea-son is that the principals never took the time to fill out the preliminary paperwork.

Introducing your company to a PPO through the PPO's online part-ner portal is like establishing a relationship with a bank. If you want to buy a million-dollar home, and you are a first-time buyer with no bank-ing history, you need to establish yourself with a bank by opening a checking account. Then you might transfer your business account to the same bank. Before long, you have a line of credit in addition to the mortgage note. With each action, you are building your history as a solid banking partner. When the time comes for the big spend, the bank happily lends you the money. They know you are in it for the long term. Making good use of the online portal is no different.

If this example sounds vaguely familiar, think back to times when you have sent queries to potential partners and received only silence in return. Did you first think to check the Internet and locate an online partner portal group? If an online partner portal was not available, did you check with the local store as Ran Slaten should have done before pitching a partnership? If the answer is no to either question, you need to do so before continuing the partnership development efforts. It will make all the difference to your business.

Navigating the Online Partner Group   The signup process for the online partner group is simple. You will fill out an electronic application, which will list you within the system. Based on your answers to the ques-tionnaire, your company will be ranked and prioritized automatically.

To begin, go to the PPO's Web site (*www.company/partner*). For in-stance, punch in *www.ibm.com/partners*. This will take you to the main page, from which you can click to the partner signup. No money re-quired, just password and profile information. Once you are established as a partner, all the other joint partnering opportunities—from events to communications—are yours to investigate.

Behind the Online Application Process: The Dirty Secret of Partner Tiering   Working with the online partner group presents no real challenges. There is, however, one wrinkle: a little known process called *tiering*. This starts when you first establish yourself as a partner and continues as your relationship progresses. In any other sport or industry, it would be called what it is: *ranking*.

Everyone has favorites, and when it comes to partners, tiering is the politically correct way of parsing the vast multitudes down to manageable numbers. Ranks, of course, are based on scores. Even firms that externally post partnerships (that is, platinum, gold, and silver partnership programs) will have an internal scoring system composed of entirely different criteria. Unfortunately, the only way to know if an internal scoring system is kept is to ask a former or current partner or employee of the PPO.

A product group in one of the most profitable companies in the world uses the following tiering system to rank partners. It relies on the information within the database to place organizations into three tiers. It is not possible to determine into which tier you will be placed at the time of company registration. Fortunately, you will be able to determine this yourself by identifying phrases, feedback, and information sent to you from the partner portal. Once "tiered," your level will not change unless you update your own information.

Tier 3:

How you are perceived internally: You are one of the pack, or to use the correct partner nomenclature, "one-too-many." The PPO is the one, and you are a part of the many.

Your peer group count: You are joined by tens of thousands of companies, all of whom have registered with the PPO.

Criteria: Your products must be compatible with the PPO's products, but don't deliver unique or custom features. Just satisfy the credit, business, and market profile characteristics and you're accepted.

Advantages: You are listed on a Web site with a product description that can provide immediate visibility to millions. You can participate in general events such as local trade shows or seminars for which the only criteria are space availability and money. Watch for mass e-mails or Web casts available to all registered partners filled with helpful but homogenous information.

Cost: There is no cost in this tier other than participation fees, but there isn't much opportunity to save money either, unless it's for early registration for attending an event.

Disadvantages: You'll receive unsolicited new product and marketing information and lots of it. Your name is likely to be sold off or given to other, bigger partners several times over. This might not be a bad thing if you are interested in creating brand awareness.

What the press will see: Third-party announcements will come in two forms. The first is a release that you would write about being a partner, and it would be true (as long as you use the correct partner nomenclature). The other type of release is written by the PPO, and your firm could be listed with a random selection of other firms. The press will not divine a particularly deep or strong relationship from either release.

Phrases that tell you the status of your company:

1. "You need to get closer to the (our) product." This means you won't move up as a partner until you make real progress in making your product line more advantageous to them.
2. "Your announcement with (competitor) didn't 'differentiate' our product." This means the PPO is unhappy with the fact that your product works as well with their competitor's product as with the PPO's own product. The PPO would like you to change this, but it is not going to come right out and say it for legal reasons. The PPO would like you to make it different, better, or at least unique if you want to get somewhere in this relationship.
3. "It would be good to invest more in our relationship." Technical efforts to improve the product are the best, but cash to put behind marketing or sales programs won't hurt.

Tier 2:

How you are perceived internally: You are somewhat unusual. You are doing some interesting things that have attracted a second look from the product group.

Your peer group count: Hundreds, and this is considered "one-too-few." For example, when you are invited to attend a seminar, you realize only 10 or 20 other companies were invited by the PPO instead of a thousand. Another clue is an invitation from the PPO to attend an internal roundtable meeting for customer or partner feedback.

Criteria: You must differentiate or optimize the partner's product or service in some unique way, or to a unique market, or both. You have been smart enough to use the PPO's product, in combination with your own product, in such a way that you have made the PPO's product infinitely better.

Advantages: You will be asked to participate in product or business forums that will provide an early jump on your competition. This is more valuable than attending a general trade show. Other marketing avenues open up as well, such as multiple listings on a company Web site as opposed to only one within the online partner group. If you suddenly appear on the list of local suppliers, it means that your company is visible within the PPO's product group. Specifically, the product group has "approved you" for working with its own sales force. This is a tremendous competitive advantage.

Cost: The cost increases in proportion to the opportunity provided, but at least it is balanced with steeper discounts for promotions. For example, the PPO asks you to participate in a national advertising campaign that would normally cost $25,000 per issue. You will participate as one of five partners highlighted by the PPO so your cost will be $5000.

Disadvantages: The PPO will constantly be looking for you to support activities beyond your firm's financial capabilities. You might not have a sales force located in multiple geographic locations to support the interest generated from the advertising campaign.

What the press will see: The press will receive a release from your firm announcing the partnership initiatives with the PPO. You're involved in the PPO's product press activities such as the press tour and the public launch.

Phrases that tell you the status of your company:

1. "The alignment of our products is much closer than before, but we still have a ways to go." Some of the PPO's desired product features are still missing. Chances are it's not something simple, like the color of the handlebar if you are a small bike manufacturer. It might be changing the handlebar material to be consistent with the other bike parts the PPO manu-

factures. Whatever the case, you better find out because it's holding up progress.

2. "We're not going to be able to have custom events until the market responds better to the solution." Either customer demand has not warranted a unique marketing event and the PPO doesn't want the entirety of the financial burden, or the PPO wants to see how much money you will put into the partnership. Either way, a stronger commitment from you is desired.

3. "I don't have authority to make the decision for X event you have requested." You might have an internal champion but not enough executive support, and your contact can't do it alone. You need to develop a relationship with an executive sponsor who can expand the scope of your relationship and the dollars your internal champion can spend on your partnership.

(**Note:** Most departments with responsibility for partnerships have a budget for partner-related press relations. PPOs tend to view press relations as a major show of support for partners due to the cost. The average internal legal review charge for a third-party press release is $2000. The average press conference with product demonstrations at a trade show is $75,000, including pre- and post-conference press follow-up and all logistical charges. Unfortunately, few companies recognize that these fees are automatically deducted from the departmental budget. A word to the wise: Be sure to validate the costs associated with the phrase "support by the PPO" and make this figure visible to your management. This adds to the return on investment/savings metrics of partnership development efforts.)

Tier 1:

How you are perceived internally: Your company is unique, a potential market leader, and a company that has captured the interest and support of multiple groups.

Your peer group count: There are typically less than 10 in any one product category and no direct competitors offering the same type of product in the same field.

Criteria: Your company must exploit the PPO's product. Specifically, you have taken the PPO's product, combined it with your own in such a way that the combination outperforms, outlasts, or is more competitively priced than any other product solution you offer. A hard bundling, product integration, or joint development proposal indicates a deep level of commitment to a partner's product line.

Advantages: There are unique and custom events between only your firm and the PPO. These events range from executive briefings to product announcements and events (trade shows and seminars) to customer advisory councils and channel programs.

Costs: Marketing and innovation efforts cost a lot of money. On the flip side, free products from the PPO are yours for the asking, as is press coverage if the PPO promotes you as a premier partner.

Disadvantages: The up-front costs associated with being a tier 1 partner can be significant.

What the press will see: The press will receive a single joint press release (release involving both companies) announcing a partnership, which includes two or more activities. The media will gauge the importance of the partnership to each firm based on the nature of the relationship as well as the title of the person quoted by the partner organization—a CEO as opposed to a product manager. Important partnerships are also identified by the geographic scope and key terms in the release, such as *an exclusive agreement,* and the type of contract signed by the companies in the partnership.

Phrases that tell you the status of your company:

1. "We have a go to market solution." Not only does this identify a unique product set, it also confirms that the joint solution is ready to be delivered to market. If the phrase "We have a first-to-market solution" is used, it means that another differentiator has been added to the partnership. It validates that the solution offered by you and the PPO is the first of its kind on the market, and by definition the first offered from the PPO. This is a point to exploit in the marketing and sales efforts.

2. "What can we do to persuade you to be our preferred partner?" Would you consider an exclusive agreement?

3. "Your product is so strategic that we want to consider all our options." If a product is truly "strategic" to a PPO, it means that it will play an integral part in helping the PPO reach its corporate objectives. Rather than waste time creating its own product, buying yours is a faster and probably cheaper way to accomplish the same goal. Get ready to talk about a potential investment or acquisition because your product may be too good.

The Central Partner Group

While the online partnering group is the first required contact in pursuing a partnership, alliance managers seeking deeper ties to a PPO head straight for the central partner group.

This group is charged with identifying, growing, and maintaining a set of partners that will encourage and increase the use of their products. In that capacity, the central partner group has two goals: one, *increase the number of partners* and two, *support the existing partners who will provide a strategic differentiator.*

The structure of the central partner division includes senior managers, industry managers, and business development managers. Partner organizations have three types of alliance or business development managers. The title *business development manager* (BDM) has recently gained favor with large companies since it blends the concepts of the sales representative who has revenue objectives and the alliance development manager. Tiering revenue and alliances is critical, and the title of business development manager ensures that this concept is reinforced. However, there are two kinds of BDMs you may meet within the central partner group:

- *Dedicated BDM:* This BDM works on specific accounts, typically three or fewer. Once your relationship is considered important enough to the PPO, you will have a BDM assigned to you, and you will become a "named" account. When you become a "strategic" partner, you will have a dedicated BDM that works full time supporting your partnership with the PPO. Another title for a named alliance manager is *depth alliance manager.*
- *Named BDM:* In this instance, you would have a BDM as your contact person, but the BDM is managing 20 to 30 companies. I've even seen a single BDM assigned to manage 50 organizations. You

aren't going to get a lot of personal attention in this scenario, but this position is still better than being one of the thousand companies who haven't even gotten to a tier 1 or tier 2 relationship. Another name for this alliance manager is *breadth alliance manager.*

This structure is transparent in a PPO's partner section on its Web site. Nonetheless, you can apply logic to deduce what category of partners might have named and dedicated managers. "Strategic alliances," of which most firms have 10 or fewer, will have named or dedicated BDMs. Separate from this are different categories of "partners" relevant to the PPO's business. These will usually have shared BDMs. The remaining hundreds or thousands of "partners" listed only in the PPO's database will not have a BDM assigned, and they would be considered tier 3 partners. The more partners in a particular category, the lower the probability of a dedicated BDM.

A common misconception is that the cost of working with a BDM in the central partner group outweighs the advantage. This is not so according to Frank Artale, formerly general manager of the NT development division at software maker Microsoft. "The BDM at Microsoft responsible for managing the VERITAS Software Microsoft partnerships is a full-time employee responsible for ensuring that Microsoft meets its commitments to VERITAS Software. This is just as the alliance manager on our side ensures that we meet our commitments to Microsoft." If neither were in place to make sure the day-to-day activities were completed, the return on investment would be far lower. Additionally, the BDM in the central partner group acts as the cog from which to direct all the other groups associated with an alliance. This often includes program managers, project managers, research, marketing, sales, training, service, support, and testing divisions that comprise the wheel of the relationship. In the absence of coordinating just one of these departments, the success of a go-to-market-solution of a tier 1 relationship is greatly reduced.

A dedicated BDM will be working along the following lines:

- Establishing the strategic direction for the relationship
- Increasing the relationship status from product-level to executive level
- Infiltrating and working with other key groups within the organization to extend the *breadth* of the partnership

- Broadening corporate-only work to field (sales) work to extend the *depth* of the partnership
- Incorporating the partner's organization into all relevant marketing programs and building campaigns unique to the partnership as well
- Facilitating the training of the customer service and support groups for better customer interaction
- Managing and reporting on the output of the relationship

If you already have a strategic relationship in place without a dedicated or shared BDM, then red flags should be flying high. Ask for a dedicated BDM to manage your partnership. If you are told no, it might be the opportunity to explore the status and future of the relationship.

The Correlation between Marketing Dollars and the Central Partner Group Ranking   The central partner group is best approached when your product is near the end or has ended its development cycle. This timing is necessary because the central partner group's focus is to create awareness and demand, which in turn generates interest and leads. In the process, the central partner group works with its partners to develop and implement "partner programs" structured in such a way as to share the cost with the partner. Even the largest PPOs are constricted by budgets that place some financial burden on their (usually smaller) partners.

The best strategy for a successful working relationship with the central partner organization is to combine budgets of one or more groups at the PPO. This will work only when you have extended the partnership to include other product groups. Prioritize your efforts to ensure that your BDM has engaged at least one other product group relevant to your business. Once the product group determines the revenue benefit to its bottom line, it will support efforts with your firm, thereby easing your financial burden. If your case is not ready for introduction to a product group, the BDM within the central partner group will be looking to you to engage in partner program activities commensurate with your tier. The translation of *participation* is often commitment to the PPO. To prepare you for this discussion and the financial expectations of the PPO, use the following market budget model.

Tier 3

If you are presently a tier 3 partner of a midsize or large company, your marketing budget just for that PPO requires the following:

1. $50,000
2. Personnel resources to participate in the PPO's events at the corporate office and some geographically dispersed locations

Tier 2

Working with a mid- or large-size firm when you become a tier 2 partner requires the following:

1. $250,000 marketing budget
2. One full-time employee for partner program management primarily dedicated to the marketing activities. Time-consuming activities include events, seminars, e-mail, and telemarketing, not to mention advertising and public relations.

Tier 1

When involved in a tier 1 partnership with a mid- or large-size firm, the requirements are increased dramatically:

1. $750,000 marketing budget
2. Two full-time employees for strategic partner programs: one alliance manager to create the strategy and build the programs and one supporting program manager who will work with the PPO's product development teams to ensure critical program dates are met
3. Two full-time marketing managers: one assigned to programs originating from the PPO's headquarters and the other responsible for managing location-based marketing programs
4. Lead management resource (part time)

It should be noted that these numbers are low for some industries such as consumer products, retail, and foods, yet are high for small consulting firms that gain sales from referral-based partnerships. For instance, if you are a two-person software gaming provider and have registered as a Sony development partner, you may be invited to attend a gaming trade show. You are notified that the cost for a small booth in Sony's partner pavilion is $2500. Doesn't sound too bad. But now add to the $2500 the cost of creating signs, booth creation and rental, setup and teardown (which at union rates is not cheap), and travel (hotel and airfare). These are the essentials of just showing up and having a presentable booth. But if you want to make the effort worthwhile and decide to promote your attendance at that show as a recognized Sony "partner," then you will have the cost of either traditional or e-mail programs, advertisement creation and placement, and press releases with associated support (even services like *BusinessWire* charge $1000 for a two-page release). Oh yes, and don't forget trade show give-away pieces: collateral material if you are cheap and water bottles or clocks if you have real money to spend. This doesn't include soft costs like the time of the personnel required to manage the show (marketing), or opportunity cost associated with these folks who could be closing business (sales). Take it one step further and put this in the broader context of ongoing marketing programs. To capitalize on the awareness created from the show, follow-up to the leads must be undertaken, and perhaps a secondary level of marketing may need to be added. This means follow-up telemarketing, direct mail, database work, and reporting before the lead is distributed to the field or channel.

Suddenly, your two-person organization has spent $40,000 of an annual budget of $50,000 on just one event. Unless you have considered all the implications of engaging with the central partner group before making a commitment, neither dollars nor personnel will be available to support programs necessary for long-term marketing partnerships.

Challenges with the Central Partner Group Assuming the financial considerations are not prohibitive, you will still run into a few barriers posed by the central partner group. First, resource constraints dictate the level of individual involvement by the partner managers at the large organization. As an example, when Microsoft decided to focus its competitive rifle on Netscape in the late nineties, it employed a campaign to migrate other independent software vendors (ISVs) from the Netscape interface to its own *Internet Explorer.* To do this, Microsoft figured it had to grow its partner list from 3000 to 15,000 in 12 months. The staff provided to accommodate this was five, both before and after the mandate.

During the same time, one group at IBM was given the goal of growing their partner group by 1000 companies. As with Microsoft, management refused to provide additional headcount to manage the increase. So at IBM, the staff of one was going to continue to "manage" its existing 350 partners without a ripple as it increased threefold.

While you might be impressed, excited, and enthusiastic when a PPO announces a "new partner program," proceed with caution. You want to be sure the program is aligned with your own objectives. If you have a good chance of being tiered in level 2 or 1, make sure you are sufficiently staffed to handle working with the partner company. If these attributes are not immediately apparent, balance opportunity with realistic payback before you jump into the new program.

Second, while partner groups are generally structured to serve large numbers of organizations, they are endowed with budgets to serve but a few. Beyond personal constraints, central marketing groups have a discretionary budget that is one tenth the size of their product group counterparts. As a result, each dollar is stretched like Gumby in order to serve the most partners. Ironically, you may have more money to spend on an initiative than the PPO will, particularly if the central partner group is relatively new or has just reorganized.

The third challenge is that your BDM is not likely to have responsibility and ownership for only one product line, application, or industry. As such, he or she won't receive credit for activities that drive revenue not directly applicable to the product line he or she manages. This has two negative consequences for your alliance efforts. On one hand, your BDM won't receive the revenue "credit" if your product line pulls through sales from another division within the PPO. This reality eliminates any motivation to introduce you to another group (partner or product equally). Conversely, BDMs of other departments aren't interested in spending the time with you since they won't get credit for revenue "already created." Ultimately, you are the one who suffers for this internal chasm.

(**Note:** In most large companies, the first BDM assigned to your account will be the individual to receive the credit for revenue your firm brings to the PPO. As BDMs are generally compensated by salary and partner-generated revenue commissions, you will increase their motivation to support your organization if you can place most of the activities and revenue under only one or two BDMs.)

It therefore becomes imperative that you work with the BDM who has responsibility and accountability for as many of your intended target groups (again, either product or partner) from the outset. If the goals shift during your relationship, don't be shy about suggesting a BDM review. Since the BDM is intended to be the cog on your relationship wheel, no one will be hurt more than you if this doesn't happen.

Navigating the Central Partner Group   Getting to the point of having a dedicated BDM is a three-step process. It starts with extending your exposure from the initial online partner group to contacting the central partner group. This can be done on the Internet as the central partner group has a URL that is generally different from the partner portal. Whereas the partner portal is *company/partner*, the central partner group will have specific attributes such as *company/partner/main*. If your product applies to many industries (light bulbs), the central partner group will be the best place to start. If you have a product squarely in a vertical market (medical equipment), it is more expedient to investigate the site *www.company/partner/healthcare*.

The next step is to identify the appropriate industry manager for your company. It is the responsibility of the industry manager (IM) to set overall group strategy and ensure that the vision is carried out through the BDMs and their partners. A number of companies list IMs on the central partner group Web site, but rarely list BDMs. If this is not available, conduct an Internet search on press releases posted by either the PPO or its partners. Many IMs are listed within the text of the press releases.

Once the IM is identified, create an e-mail or voice mail pitch using compelling data points: number of *their* product units leveraged through *your* channel, potential increased market penetration enabled by your firm, and level of marketing dollars allocated to spend on partner initiatives.

Stay clear of the BDM until the industry manager is contacted. You want to start as high as possible in the decision-making food chain before working out the details of the relationship. It's important to remember that the industry manager is not traditionally compensated by commission: The main objective of the role is to anticipate strategically the long-term needs of the product group. Thus, the IM position is diametrically opposed to that of the commission-based, short-term-focused BDM.

Additionally, compared with the BDM, the IM is going to have access to a larger piece of the budgetary pie as well as more visibility and influence with executives. Once you and the industry manager have aligned the value of a partnership between your two firms, the BDM becomes vital to building the partner programs and extending your work throughout the PPO.

The Product Group

This group is responsible for bringing new products to market and achieving revenue goals associated with the product line(s). The group accomplishes these objectives using the following means:

- Understanding the target market needs
- Defining the product feature set
- Working with the development group to create the product
- Identifying any holes that are left in the solution
- Establishing partnerships with firms that can provide products to fill in the holes in their solution

The *product manager* (PM) is the individual directly responsible for the product line business. Guided by product release timelines, PMs are rarely informed by development of the gap between their intended product and that which is getting ready to roll off the production line. Unfortunately for the PM, the marketing machine is already in action, the sales force has been briefed and the service and support organizations are in training. Under pressure to stay on schedule, product groups must fill the product gap, and this is made possible through partnerships.

This situation places your firm in a position of strength if you can take advantage of the environment by firmly erecting large competitive barriers as you portray yourself as the player in the PPO's next product development cycle. You will also be in a better position to negotiate a valuable agreement.

The organizational structure of product groups tends to be accomplished by placing a product group within a business unit. For instance, American Express has eight separate business divisions. Its financial services products for the small-business owner are created within one group while products for large institutions are created and delivered by another. The partnerships required to deliver or market these products are managed by

BDMs within each business unit. Depending on the size of a product line, an individual PM will be responsible for one or two products while a *group product manager* (GPM) is responsible for many product lines.

(**Note:** The title *program manager* is frequently applied to many roles in marketing, product development, consulting, and even sales implementation. In large companies, program managers are usually in a group parallel to the product group. Whereas product managers are responsible for identifying, delivering, and marketing a product, program managers work with the actual engineers, researchers, or other personnel responsible for actually making the product. As such product managers receive information about product gaps from their program manager counterparts, they then must find and create a partnership. Together, product and program managers bring a product to market. For your partnership development purpose, the product manager is the decision maker.)

The most common types of partnerships created by PMs are distribution and joint development. Yet the product group heavily influences joint marketing partnerships created within the central partner group and joint sales partnerships created in the field sales organization. It is also the PM's responsibility to determine the validity of an investment or acquisition by the PPO's corporate development into your firm. All of these partnerships can strengthen your product's position in the marketplace while only a few have a real, immediate, and direct impact on revenue and shareholder value. To the degree that the PM believes your company is truly strategic, he or she will also engage executives within the PPO to "sponsor" or promote and support your firm throughout the PPO at the executive level.

As the central point of partnership decision making, product managers possess a unique *circle of influence* (Figure 7–1). Because of this, I consider them the best point of entry for significant partnership development efforts.

When to Approach the Product Group   Product groups within large companies are ideal to approach when your product has been validated in the marketplace by customers or other partners. This doesn't necessarily mean that you must have a completed product. It simply means your product has been placed in the hands of customers and has received positive feedback. A high comfort level is all that's required to engage the product group in a partnership discussion.

Figure 7–1   Circle of Influence for a Decision Maker

If your product is on the market and you have recognized overlapping or competitive areas with the PPO's products, you have another valid reason to approach the PPO. The intent of the partnership is to determine if either side is willing to explore changes (that is, removing its source of competition) in exchange for a better market position for both products.

In the process of either, product group discussion can yield stimulating ideas for future products and strategies. If you are considering a new market or product diversification built on the PPO's products, you will need to identify how to make the two products work together in a blended, seamless fashion. This is called *joint development*: two companies working jointly on a customer problem that can be solved through a new product. It doesn't matter if the actual problem is solved by one group or both, or if money transfers hands. The fact that two firms have come together to solve a common customer problem sends a very significant message to the marketplace.

Challenges with the Product Groups   Product groups are the most challenging group to navigate. PMs coordinate their program manager peers as well as internal marketing departments responsible for lead generation and promotion. PMs support sales to address product-related customer issues, develop new products, and create long-term product plans, and they also coordinate the vendors and suppliers responsible for delivering raw materials.

PMs have an inordinate level of responsibility and wield an amazing level of power within major corporations. With the profit and loss directly attributable to a product line, a single PM may have millions of dollars to spend on partnership programs.

Yours Is Only the 146,001st E-mail of the Year! Of all the barriers associated with the product group, you can do nothing about a PM's lack of available time. Even in a thriving economy, product groups are lean operations. A few examples offer a glimpse into the workplace realities of a PM:

- PMs at a *Fortune 50* firm receive an average of 400 pieces of e-mail per day:
  - Totaling 146,000 pieces of e-mail per year
- PMs receive an average of 50 voice mails per day:
  - Totaling 13,000 voice mails per year
  - Response times to voice mails are two weeks on average
- Group product managers receive nearly 1000 pieces of e-mail per day, 600 originating internally
- Group product managers receive an average of 200 voice mails per day:
  - Totaling 73,000 voice mails per year

Now take a look at the time in the day a product manager has to get their work done.

Meetings	4 hours
Planning	1 hour
Product or program efforts	2 hours
E-mails	1 hour at best, 3 at worst
Return phone calls	2 hours
Manage existing partners	1 hour
Total	11- to 14-hour day

Where does "prospective partner work" fit into this day? It doesn't, and that's the problem.

Culture Shock   Culture also plays a big role in the actions of the product team. For example, computer manufacturer Hewlett-Packard doesn't promote answering the phone. It's not that the employees are working from home or are unavailable or that they don't care. It's just that "if a person wants you, he or she can either send an e-mail or leave a message," as one product manager said. "I can't risk answering," to take the time to "qualify the opportunity and educate the caller," he said. To summarize the philosophy, a second PM figured that "if they are really important, they'll have my e-mail address and send me something."

Burnout rates are high within product groups at large companies, which results in a challenge for outsiders in dealing with employee turnover. Imagine the stress from endless meetings, customer and partner demands, and internal politics compounded with the constant irritation of managing correspondence associated with daily work. Now add the impact of employee turnover either out of the company or to another group. Many companies reorganize every six months, and some even have job change restrictions barring product managers from shifting positions until the next reorganization. During these periods, a lot of shifting occurs as people move up, over, or out of the group. The result is an elimination of a partner opportunity with the elimination of the decision maker. If you haven't been aware of possible changes and anticipated the impact, you will have to start over with new decision makers with a different agenda.

In one case, one of my clients had created a consulting service for small-business retailers to offer Web site creation services. In the middle of 1996, this was a hot commodity. The PPO was a multi-billion dollar franchise firm that desired to test it out on its own franchises. If they could do it without much hassle, then it had a chance of rolling out across the country to the other 4500 franchises. After a few meetings, the PM at the PPO had assembled 15 franchise owners in the room for a four-hour seminar. The results showed that over half of those in the room had caught the vision and made immediate plans to go out on sales calls with our client right then and there. After initial sales had been made, the PM was armed with a 50 percent response from his customers (the franchise owners), and he made plans to roll out a national program.

On a Friday I confirmed to our client that the national rollout program was in development and would be rolled out within the month. The following Monday I had to call back and retract my words. The PM had just informed me that he was taking a position within another product group at his own company and would not be able to carry our initiative forward. While the new manager might be inclined to continue, it was not guaranteed.

To avoid this type of situation, get as close to the PM as soon as possible so he or she will feel compelled to give you an indication if he or she moves out of that role.

Anticipating Employee Turnover Cycle   One way to reduce risk associated with turnover is to time partner decisions between the six-month reorganizations. You can find out where you are in the cycle by asking the organization when they have reviews (every six months or every year). This knowledge will help you plan the following cycle:

Month 1: Dust settles, roles are defined.

Month 2: Plans are created and ramping up.

Months 3 and 4: Work is getting done, partnerships are being started.

Month 5: Agreements are being created, reviews are being written.

Month 6: Reviews are being written, and talks are being closed or stalled until the next cycle

Incorporate this time frame into your program timelines even as you are preparing to navigate the maze of the product group. Also, get agreements in writing as soon as possible. "If we don't get the agreement signed before the turnover happens, all our work is lost," said Steve Volkers, director of business development for The Nature Conservancy. "It's the number 1 motivator for us to get things done quickly. You just never know when a change will happen."

The Hazards in "Going Too High"   The best way to kill your relationship with a product manager is by approaching a senior-level executive within the product group. This is known as "going too high," and it will severely slow down your progress. Mike Walsh, CEO and president of design sharing manufacturer Actify Corporation, believes that sometimes you have to go around or above someone but "never never" in the beginning of the partnership development process. "Large companies are designed to push down responsibility and accountability to lower-level managers so they are essentially running their own businesses." If you start with the executive, you are going to simultaneously irritate the product manager who will make the final decision and waste a silver-bullet contact on an inconsequential discussion.

At the same time, starting with a junior-level product manager is going to relegate you into the quagmire of tactical discussions. People who are individual-contributor-level or low-level managers tend to be slow, methodological, and process oriented. Continued Walsh, "They are not known to take risks, or else they'd be higher in the organization." The result is that you are stuck on a steam engine when you need to be on the bullet train. You can't go too high, but you can't go too low either. You have to find the product manager in the middle that is strategic enough to think ahead and tactical enough to get things done. Finally, this person "must be endowed with the authority to write the check and stand on the podium when the agreement is signed," concluded Walsh.

Nowhere in the organization is this more important than with the product group, where manager, senior manager, lead manager, group manager, group product manager, director of product management, vice president of product management, and then general manager can all reside.

Navigating the Maze of the Product Group   Entry to the product groups comes after identifying which product group to attack. The first shortcut is to purchase organizational charts (if available) created by third-party firms. While this information can be expensive in the short term (from $1000 to $3000 per year with quarterly updates) and only drills down to the director level, it is well worth the money.

One example is Directions on Microsoft (*www.directionsonmicrosoft. com*). This firm is staffed by ex-Microsoft employees who make a substantial living by doing nothing more than tracking Microsoft's every move. It is a godsend to anyone who has spent more than an hour looking on the Web site trying to identify the right product group to contact.

If this is hard to come by, assess the organization's Web site. Search the press releases posted by the targeted product group within the PPO. A PM is invariably listed within the text. From that point it's just a matter of when to initiate a voice or e-mail introduction. Knowing that communication preferences and cultures vary from PPO to PPO, don't rely exclusively on e-mail or voice mail. Use both.

If you are determined to "go high," one consistency I've noticed is that the higher the title within an organization, the faster the response to e-mails. On the whole, senior executives at *Fortune 50* organizations are on e-mail Sunday nights from 9 to 11 P.M.; after the kids have gone to bed. Clients are continually surprised when I encourage their late-night Sunday correspondence, but they are gratified when a response is returned within 10 minutes.

If none of the foregoing methods works, it's time to become a little sneaky and use a PPO's customer support software against itself. All large companies employ software intended to direct incoming e-mails received through a Web site. The routing of the e-mail depends on key words contained within the e-mail text. It is not uncommon for the routing rules to send "product-related questions" directly to product managers. Our own internal customer support software has me assigned as the contact for inquiries from corporate venture groups. Just last week a question was routed to me from a principal with the Boeing Venture Group who was interested in hiring us to help their portfolio companies create partnerships. Direct requests work!

Yet another avenue by which you can enter the product group is the sales or marketing representatives in the field. The strategy is to articulate a value proposition that makes a difference to the salesperson's pocketbook. This is the financial case of a potential partnership. However, you need just one conversation with the product group to verify some details to confirm how the products will work together in a particular situation. This gives the sales rep incentive to either find or forward you to the right PM at the corporate office.

If the salesperson doesn't return your initial call quickly, contact the marketing representative with a "new marketing opportunity." A call back from this tactic is likely since it's the job of the marketing liaison to investigate all reasonable opportunities. In the process, marketing personnel will often disseminate information without asking questions you might not be able to answer. If you don't have a completed financial case for a partnership or you are unsure if the value proposition is strong enough for a partnership, contacting the field marketing representative is less risky than contacting the sales rep, and it can yield the same result—the name of the PM.

If you are still having no luck identifying the right contact at the product group, don't be shy about contacting the media. With more contacts than most Rolodex-stuffed BDMs, members of the press are sometimes interested in helping if it will benefit their ability to capture a newsworthy story in the future. To be successful, frame the query under the topic of "strategic relationship." Be careful to position the interest as introductory in nature as opposed to existing discussions. Who knows? You might even get a bit of free insight as to internal politics, reorganizations, and upcoming activities. Just be sure to remember the source when the time comes to announce the deal.

The Corporate Development Group

Corporate development groups exist to negotiate and close deals that are going to forward the financial position of the company. Matt Frymier, Bank of America's principal manager of the venture group, provides a perspective common among corporate venture groups. "We look at companies where we can use their product internally but also extend to our partners. If we can make money as this is used by the outside world, then it's a bonus." Don Paul, CIO of Chevron and president of the Chevron Venture Group, has a slightly different philosophy. "We are primarily interested in companies who can bring us products and services that will improve our efficiency. The end result of this is a more profitable outcome for the organization." And if a solution can be used externally for customers, that's fine, but "it's not the primary motivation for investment or acquisition."

The organizational structure of corporate development departments tends to be consistent among large companies. Corporate development resides within the finance or operations division. Corporate development managers are responsible for approving and writing deals while the finance managers are responsible for conducting the financial analysis on each deal. For PPOs with product groups not located at corporate headquarters, corporate development will often place an on-site corporate development manager.

Intel is a good example of a headquarter-based corporate development organization with field-based managers. With research and development product groups around the world, Intel realized it was missing out on opportunities to invest and acquire new technologies. After placing corporate development managers in the field, the quality, nature, and return increased dramatically.

When to Approach the Corporate Development Group   When a partnership exists between two companies, one or both are probably considering ways to maximize the return on future efforts. This is the best time to approach corporate development because an outside company has established itself within the PPO, it has built a track record of performance, and it is supported by at least one product group. According to Kris Hagerman, executive vice president of strategic operations at VERITAS Software, no investment or acquisition opportunity is even considered before a relationship is established with the product side of the house. A good many publicly held companies have guidelines requiring an existing relationship with the product group before an M&A transaction is considered.

If you don't yet have a formal partnership with a PPO, "always call the alliance group first," advises Hagerman. "Until a company has a business relationship, the possibility that a merger or acquisition activity will happen is inconceivable. The present acquisition opportunities we are considering are those with whom we already have an established relationship. This is 100 percent true on the venture investment side."

If a competitor has received an investment from a PPO, it is a signal that the PPO might be interested in spreading its financial risk among several companies in the same product category. This is particularly true when you have a new product in a new industry. One example is the new product category of cloning within the biotechnology industry. Pharmaceutical firms with corporate development groups aren't sure which firm will be the clear winner, so they choose to invest in multiple organizations.

The same holds true for becoming the target of an acquisition. If you have a new product in a new market category, you might be ripe for an acquisition from a PPO with a product diversification strategy. A third time to approach the corporate development group of a PPO is when you identify partnerships, investments, or acquisitions happening among the PPO's primary competitors. If your solution can help block a competitive move by the PPO's nemesis, you have a strategic case that has less to do with return on investment for your solution than with a high return on investment for the overall position and return of the PPO.

Challenges Associated with Corporate Development Corporate development organizations have bandwidth constraints similar to product groups. For controlling such seemingly vast amounts of money, the personnel team is stretched. Managing incoming calls, proposals, and e-mails causes delays longer than those from the product groups—more than a month on average for a response of any kind.

As an example, chip maker Intel has a vast array of product groups of interest to entrepreneurs. Its investments and acquisitions are in a range that includes security, digital cameras, biometrics, wireless, networking, even television components. For this reason, engineers and inventors around the world are contacting the corporate development department. Over 100 proposals a day just for acquisitions are received at each of its corporate development offices. But fewer than 10 percent are reviewed by a corporate development manager. Of these, fewer than 5 percent of these make it to the product groups for secondary review.

The fact that they have a criteria and your firm doesn't fit it is a complete wild-card obstacle. In one situation a PPO identified that it wanted to purchase only those firms greater than $40 million in revenue but less than $100 million. The acquisition candidate needed to have a market product line focused on a specific vertical industry and preferably be the dominant player in that market. Further, the firm didn't necessarily need to be an independent product vendor. It could be a consulting firm that would provide the acquiring company "immediate market dominance," or at least the path to achieve that goal.

While it is nearly impossible for your firm to have this type of inside knowledge about a PPO, the wisdom of being "in the right place at the right time with the right business case" is truly a reality of business. It is up to you to determine the opportunity cost of the challenge and potential home run of an investment or acquisition.

Navigating the Corporate Development Group   Navigating corporate development is not difficult. In fact, corporate development can be reached quickly by calling the main number of a PPO and asking for this division. Alternatively, you can go directly to a Web site to access the corporate development group (*www.company/ventures.com*).

The corporate development group for Intel, for example, provides one of the most detailed sites for your investment or acquisition efforts (*www.intel.com/capital*). In addition to providing money, Intel identifies the other services investees can expect after the investment is completed. The site also provides the strategic goals of the corporate development group and a venue in which to submit a proposal. Intel cautions that while it "will promptly acknowledge receipt of the proposal, it may take up to four weeks to process your request."

This time frame for receiving an answer is going to be about the same duration as if you had placed a direct call into the corporate development group. In either case, the process and individuals are usually consistent. An administrator will pick up the line and provide the relevant information of where to send the solicitations. Assistants complete first-level reviews that determine the basics: investment or acquisition, product category, criteria alignment with posted information, and registration with the online partner group. This screening effort cuts the group down to 10 percent. Secondary reviewers within corporate development, usually the corporate development manager, will take anywhere from a week to a month to read the plan. If it passes this stage, it is sent to the appropriate product manager.

This last point can be a bottleneck. One, it assumes that corporate development knows the right product manager. In a 3000-person organization this might be a reasonable expectation. In a 50,000-person organization, it is not. Corporate development organizations are going to spend some time mucking around to find the right person just as you would.

Since a PM out of the product group is going to be responsible for making the final decision, I advise working the product development group in parallel. This is the best way to collapse time frames in either investment or acquisition efforts. As corporate development uncovers synergistic areas strategic to the entire PPO, the product group may be validating the integrity and alignment of the product set. Both organizations can arrive at the same conclusion faster and perhaps more efficiently than if you pursued one or the other department in isolation.

CHAPTER

8

Structuring Partnership Agreements

CHAPTER HIGHLIGHTS

- *Moving from a trust-based partnership to a formal agreement*
- *Deal term inversion*
- *Deal break fees by agreement type*

The Strength of the Word

WHEN THE BASQUES CREATED PARTNERSHIPS with kings, traders, and enemies alike under the oak tree in Guernica, the decision was invariably made as to the necessity of a written document. The Basques considered their word and their honor one and the same, so a written document was irrelevant once a final deal had been made. If a written document was prepared, it was solely for the comfort and requirements of their partner. Even today, not much has changed these attitudes for some people. One of my first clients insisted on nothing more than a handshake deal, using the famous line that he was "as good as his word." He trusted that I could perform and, in turn, I trusted he would pay. For five months, our firms worked jointly on an effort without payment to either side. Yet we shared a vision, a common goal, and we were going to put all reasonable resources necessary to achieve that goal. When the project was successfully concluded, our fees were paid, and the trust-based relationship with this firm continues today, after five years.

Trust-Based Partnerships

How do you determine if your partnership is one that could succeed without an agreement, particularly in our seemingly litigious climate? Very simply. By determining the level of trust within the partnership and balancing this with the climate and culture of the partners. Sole proprietor Shandel Slaten has verbal contracts with two firms that produce nearly 50 new potential customers a month, instead of the handful she creates alone. Midsize hay manufacturing firm Anderson Hay and Grain has grown from $10 to $95 million in five years using verbal contracts for its marketing and distribution arrangements. Anderson's firm existed for 35 years without a single agreement, a policy that changed only recently when one was created for a distribution partner. *Fortune 500* companies VERITAS Software and Microsoft Corporation invested millions of dollars in a global marketing, sales, and product partnership after a single meeting between the CEOs and their verbal commitment to one another. It wasn't until after two years of multinational work that the two firms considered creating a formal contract.

In all cases, written agreements were not considered necessary to achieving revenue-based results. Former Microsoft general manager Frank Artale summed up the general consensus: "When both individuals recognize a market opportunity and agree on the best means to move forward, they commit their organizations to the effort." The results either graduate the nature of the effort or nullify it over time.

Trust-based partnerships typically start with implementing regional sales or customer-based programs. The individual firms were probably operating on a local basis, and the products they offered probably did not need to be adapted in any way before partnership work began.

A natural evolution from sales to marketing trust-based partnerships occurs when sales success stories are reproduced in marketing literature. With marketing efforts localized, expenditures and personnel resources can be controlled if they are under the radar of the corporate marketing group. This is advantageous when the products overlap or if the corporate positioning of the firms is not entirely complementary.

Another benefit of flying under the corporate radar is the ability to leverage your partner's sales or distribution network. Localized efforts rarely require national program involvement, eliminating the necessity to be registered or certified at a national level.

Moving from a Trust-Based Partnership to a Formal Agreement

Some trust-based partnerships continue for years without requiring any sort of formal agreement. Others evolve into formally recognized partnerships. This occurs when the partnership has graduated from a sales- or marketing-oriented partnership to one that includes product development. When both firms are investing their new product development efforts to the benefit of the partner, a formal partnership agreement reduces risks.

One such example is the partnership between boat lift manufacturer Sunstream Corporation and recreational boat maker Cobalt Corporation. Neither firm felt it necessary to bind its field sales enterprise with a formal agreement. When the CEOs desired to capture a new consumer boat market with a jointly designed product, each firm dedicated a portion of its engineering team to the new effort. This investment in personnel was followed by a capital investment in materials. The monetary value of the investment was the motivating factor toward creating a joint design and development agreement.

Market dynamics and management changeovers have the power to abruptly alter partnerships. To protect his firm, CEO Mark Blumenthal of Blumenthal Uniforms utilized a distribution and licensing agreement with a supplier in the event that there would be sudden contract cancellations brought about by a management change. To protect her France Luxe brand of hair accessories against competitors, The Finest Accessories CEO Laurie Erickson had her key manufacturing partners sign an exclusive agreement. This was in response to a situation in which a long-time manufacturing partner had agreed to create a product for a competitor using a design process Erickson created. In each of these instances, all of the partner CEOs continue to feel they have trust-based relationships with their partners. But their dependence on their partners had increased so dramatically that they needed to be mentally and legally assured, even for extreme unforeseen events.

Having moved past the stage of a trust-based partnership, structuring partner agreements highlights a more formal relationship between companies. This chapter is a contract walk-through, in which the agreements used for the primary partnerships are broken down into their most important parts. Outside the main body of the contract are exhibits and addenda, also useful to extending an existing partnership while avoiding the hassle of a creating a completely new agreement. Armed with this knowledge, you are prepared to voice the agreement terms and conditions you desire early on in the process. This sets the expectations for your partner, which in turn reduces the negotiation cycles.

Partnership Agreements Defined

For those of you who cannot comprehend conducting business without the use of a formally recognized partnership, you have two options. The first is to use an informal or non-legally binding partnership agreement as recognition that a partnership "is in the process" of being created. The second option is to wait and create a formal partnership with a legally binding partnership and an associated agreement.

Informal partnerships and their agreements are used primarily as a means to motivate the creation of a formal or definitive written partnership agreement. Since creating a simple press release between companies can take up to three months as in the case of Microsoft and VERITAS Software, using an informal agreement simply provides a level of comfort to both entities. With this in place, both firms acknowledge each is working diligently toward a formal agreement without artificially slowing down the efforts of either firm.

Informal Partnerships

This preagreement category is recognized in only three types of documents: a letter of intent (LOI), a heads of agreement (HOA), and a memorandum of understanding (MOU). The intent of each document is to create a non-legally binding framework that provides each party defined objectives to complete in a specified period of time.

For instance, once completing the due-diligence phase for a joint development agreement (JDA), you might want to create an LOI that states when a formal JDA will be completed. While not including the price, terms, or conditions of the agreement itself, the letter signals that both firms are working toward the goal of a mutually agreeable outcome.

A common concern raised by novice alliance managers is that the use of an informal agreement will delay the completion of a formal partnership. On the contrary, utilizing an LOI, MOU, or HOA actually accelerates the partnership negotiation discussions. By requiring a partnership to be formally recognized within a stated period of time, both entities realize that the clock has begun to tick and that they have a limited amount of time to create a formal agreement. Otherwise, each firm might pursue other alternatives, and all the efforts toward this partnership would be lost.

Using the word *informal* in the context of these agreements identifies the lack of penalty or recourse available to either party should the final agreement not be reached. In the majority of instances, these agreements are no more than one-page letters signed by representatives from each firm.

Choosing among an LOI, HOA, or MOU   The differences within the three informal agreements are very subtle and are sometimes more dependent on a company culture than common use. For instance, a letter of intent is the most generic informal agreement, and it signifies nothing more than an attempt to have an agreement at a specific point in time.

Compare this to a heads of agreement, which is generally used to establish executive support to employees, vendors, customers, and suppliers. It positions two firms as having a relationship at the executive level as opposed to the more menial product, marketing, or sales level. As a result, HOAs are viewed as a precursor to a broader and deeper strategic relationship. Given this positioning, sales executives are quick to leverage this announcement in order to close customer orders reliant upon two companies working together.

In one example, two software application providers created a heads-of-agreement letter to assist the efforts of the sales personnel. At the time, each company was consistently being blocked out of competitive selling situations by rivals who had partnered to sell a joint product solution. The heads of agreement allowed the two firms to present their solution as a package, and the entities as partners. This leveled the playing field without requiring costly product integration.

A memorandum of understanding is more often used when a partnership includes product-level programs. While still a precursor to a final agreement, specific elements about product integration, development, support, or service are included in the MOU. This requires the product group to set aside resources in advance of a formal agreement, indicating a commitment to execute upon deliverables.

Recently a service organization for retired CEOs created a memorandum of understanding with a large consulting organization. The MOU was used to acknowledge that the retired executives were available to the consulting firm. As the marketing work commenced, so did the formal process of creating a revenue sharing agreement between the two organizations.

Constructing Informal Agreements The three informal partnerships mentioned have associated agreements. The construction of the letter of intent (LOI), heads of agreement (HOA), and memo of understanding (MOU) is very similar. In the majority of instances, these agreements are one-page letters signed by representatives from each firm.

The five aspects required in each of the documents include the products under discussion, the terms and conditions, due-diligence terms, time frame, and conduct of business. In both the LOI and HOA, the products under discussion are normally listed in a paragraph form. In an MOU, the products are listed in a more formal definitions section. An interactive gaming software provider working with a telecommunications firm used the following definitions in its MOU:

1. *"[Solution name]" refers to [firm name's] interactive gaming software, which is a browser-based, interactive software with wireless capabilities.*
2. *"Licensed content" refers to content that has been licensed to either [firm name] or [partner name].*
3. *"Global networking services" refers to the [partner's name] offerings of data centers, equipment, software, and support required to host and deliver applications online and wirelessly.*

The terms and conditions section within the LOI and HOA is limited in scope. Typically it contains a one- or two-sentence statement about the intent of the future agreement. One LOI for a joint development agreement between a two-person consumer foods company and a large retail chain reads as follows:

> *[Retail chain] and [consumer foods company] intend to create a joint development agreement for the creation of a new candy product to be branded under [retail chain] name.*

Contrast this with the terms and conditions in the MOU for the gaming and telecommunications provider:

1. *[Gaming company] will be the exclusive provider of online interactive gaming software application for the [partner] channel (Exhibit A).*
2. *[Partner] will be the exclusive provider of global networking services to [gaming company] internally (Exhibit C).*
3. *[Gaming company] will offer and bundle [partner] to its customers (Exhibit D).*
4. *Length of the agreement will be for three years with an option to renew for an additional two (2) years based on performance measurements to be determined for the final agreement.*
5. *[Partner] will pay [gaming company] for a custom [partner] gaming user interface, content conversion, software licensing, and management fee (Exhibit E).*
6. *[Gaming company] will pay [company] fees for hosting network services (Exhibit E).*
7. *[Partner] and [gaming company] will share the revenue for [partner] customers' utilizing the [gaming company] software (Exhibit F).*

The next section, due-diligence review, then identifies what, if any, items are to be turned over for review. The standard paragraph used for most agreements, whether it's a distribution agreement or an agreement that includes an investment, reads as follows:

> *The [agreement type] is subject to the satisfactory completion of a due-diligence review by [partner name]. [Your firm] will make available to [partner] such product, customer and internal documentation, relevant design documents, design specifications, databases, preliminary patent filings, and information as [partner] reasonably requests, so that [partner] can perform a full investigation of [your firm's] product, business, and legal conditions.*

Using the technical and financial due-diligence matrices will aid in identifying which of the requests are reasonable for your situation. Don't hesitate to eliminate elements that overstep the intent of your partnership.

The time frame for the completion of an agreement ranges from a simple sentence stating the agreement due date to a more complex time-frame statement. The complex statement is usually found in an MOU and is called a *definitive agreement* statement:

> ***Definitive Agreement(s).*** *The terms and provisions of the [agreement name] will be contained in Definitive Agreement(s) in a form customary in transactions of this type and satisfactory to both [your firm] and [partner]. The terms and provisions shall include, among others, representations, warranties, and covenants of [your firm] and customary conditions of Closing. Each party agrees to use its best efforts to sign a Definitive Agreement(s) and close the transactions contemplated thereby no later than December 23, 2002.*

When creating an informal agreement, your partner will either encourage you to continue normal business operations or to refrain from pursuing new business or partner opportunities. The latter is more problematic to young firms who live and die by each customer order. If this delay is requested, define what "normal business operations" means. I would encourage you to separate new sales from new types of partners. The intent of this term is to avoid adding infrastructure to your company today that might ultimately turn into the new partner's burden tomorrow.

The best course of action is to use the following paragraph, named the *conduct-of-business clause*, which does not hinder existing business practices. Rather, it requires you to consult with the partner first. This provides visibility to the partner, thereby reducing your risk of opportunities lost as well as the partner's risk of your entering into an imprudent business venture:

> ***Conduct of Business.*** *From the date hereof until the earlier of (i) the cessation of discussions between [your firm] and [partner], (ii) the execution of the Definitive Agreements, or (iii) the Termination Time, [your firm] will conduct its business in the normal and ordinary course, consistent with prior practices, and will also consult with [partner] on an ongoing basis*

regarding its business activities undertaken in the ordinary course, includ-
ing without limitation, any license agreements (other than standard end-
user license agreements), OEM agreements, "bundling" agreements, or
other material contracts into which [your firm] proposes to enter.

Formal Operations Agreements

The content and structure of all four types of operations agreements
closely resemble a memo of understanding. Each agreement includes
the partner intent (definitions), deliverables (terms and conditions),
review and approval process (due diligence), monies, and timelines. The
primary addition to these agreements that sets them apart from the
informal agreements concerns the ownership of any intellectual property created during the partnership.

This stipulation is common in the manufacturing and engineering
agreements, but sometimes appears in the facilities and land agreements as well. The ownership rights and associated revenue derived from
new innovations resulting from an agreement must be set forth within
the contract.

This is accomplished by stating product ownership within the definitions section (also called *recitals* depending on the company and industry). One financial services company included the following recital
in its operations agreement:

> *[Financial services company] solely owns and operates a Small Business-*
> *oriented portal on the World Wide Web currently titled "[name]" and*
> *currently accessible through the URL http://www.[name].com, which*
> *displays information and content intended for Small Businesses and pro-*
> *vides, promotes, and sells products and services to Small Businesses (such*
> *portal, together with any successor URL or portal, the "[site name]").*
> *Among these services are [explicit services listed].*

This statement was supported by a secondary section on the ownership
of new products to be created between the financial services firm and
its engineering partner:

> **Ownership by [financial firm].** *All rights, including all Intellectual*
> *Property Rights, in all engineering delivery processes ("Processes") cre-*

ated by [financial firm] or [engineering firm] in connection with the Agreement and the provision of the Custom Services shall be the sole and exclusive property of [financial firm] and, to the extent that such Processes embody or are reflected in Work Product, such Work Product shall be considered "works made for hire" under the United States copyright laws. In the event any such Work Product or Processes does not fall within the specifically enumerated works that constitute "works made for hire" under the United States copyright laws or the ownership of all of the Intellectual Property Rights in and to any such Work Product or Processes does not vest, solely and exclusively, in [financial firm] pursuant to the previous sentence, Agent hereby agrees to assign and, upon their authorship or creation (or upon the Effective Date, whichever occurs later), expressly and automatically assigns all Intellectual Property Rights in and to such Work Product and Processes to [financial firm]. From time to time, upon [financial firm] request, [engineering firm] shall confirm such assignments by execution and delivery of such assignments, confirmations, or other written instruments as [financial firm] may request. Further, to the extent [engineering firm] has any so called "moral rights" in and to such Work Product or Processes that cannot be assigned to [financial firm], [engineering firm] hereby unconditionally and irrevocably waives the enforcement of all such moral rights, and all claims and causes of action of any kind with respect to any of the foregoing, whether now known or hereafter devised. To the extent such rights cannot be waived, [engineering firm] hereby grants to [financial firm] a perpetual, irrevocable, exclusive, worldwide, royalty-free, unrestricted right and license to use, execute, reproduce, distribute, sell copies of, modify, create derivative works of, publicly perform and publicly display, with the right to sublicense and assign such moral rights in and to such Work Product or Processes, including without limitation, the right to use in any way whatsoever the Work Product or Processes in any and all media now known or hereafter devised.

Licensing and Distribution Agreements

Alliance managers almost always ask me to describe the difference between the various licensing and distribution terms. They also usually ask me to clarify the reasonable terms to include in each agreement. I typically provide a list of terms that gives the relevance and likelihood that the term will be used in an agreement (Table 8–1).

The distribution agreement matrix is particularly useful as it identifies why a particular term is important to one party and not so important to

Table 8–1   Distribution Agreement Matrix

Requested Term	Licensing	Soft Bundling	Hard Bundling	Private Labeling
Brand name importance.	Very important to both.	Very important; usually given.	Moderate to the smaller partner; critical to the larger partner.	Hard to get for partner whose product is not visible to the customer.
Logo usage.	Critical to the small partner; important to the larger partner.	Very important to both.	Moderate to the smaller partner, very important to the larger partner.	Rare for the embedded product unless it is a large, established firm.
Packaging.	Critical to both.	Very important to both.	Usually the larger partner will dominate this, and the smaller partner has little if any control.	Smaller partner will have no say. Larger partner will determine all.
Promotion.	Critical to the smaller partner; only moderately important to larger partner unless partnership and product are key to its solution.	Critical to smaller partners; moderate for larger partner.	Critical for smaller partner as it will boost credibility; moderate for larger partner.	Embedded product must handle its own promotion if not prevented by the agreement.
Payments.	Standard schedules for up-front, ongoing, and discounts.	Usually no payment for soft bundling. Each company accepts sales separately.	Company including its product in the bundle (usually the larger) will send payment to the smaller firm.	Company including private labeling sends the check.
Up-front payments.	Depends on industry.	Almost never.	Sometimes.	Almost always.
Guarantees.	Depends on quantities promised, industry, and competition.	Never.	Sometimes but are usually only for 12 months or less.	Almost always and usually for 1–3 years.
Flat fees.	Sometimes; usually given from large companies to small companies.	Almost never.	Sometimes. Can be small to large companies or vice versa.	Depends on the opportunity and cost for both parties.
Scale royalty fees.	Many times where both parties are of moderate or large size.	Never.	Sometimes.	Almost always.
Support.	Varies.	Each company supports its own product.	Most of the time support is provided by the company licensing the product.	Support is always provided by the company private labeling the product.

the other. Unfortunately, when it comes to hard bundling and OEM agreements, it is the larger of the two organizations that has a particular advantage. Understanding what this means for your company enables you to create and propose a reasonable alternative term.

Five Critical Components for Licensing and Distribution   Similar to the operations agreement, licensing and distribution agreements (LDAs) include the up-front recitals and definitions. However, unlike those documents, the terms and conditions are much too lengthy to include in a single list. Instead, each term is given its own section and where needed, subsections. As a result, LDAs are easily 20 pages in length.

The most important and touchy sections in this type of agreement are licensing grant, performance measurements, termination, customer support clauses, and disclosure and/or discussion with other parties. Each has been responsible for placing a great many partnerships in the courtroom, usually for compensation lost as a result of a failed partnership. Your ability to define the sections according to your needs will keep the partnership on track.

1. *Licensing Grants*   The first section of note in the LDA is the license grant. This section identifies exactly what products are being licensed and what rights the company licensing the products (the licensee) has under the agreement.

A simple license agreement for a consulting services provider who is licensing its methodologies to a partner reads as follows:

> *[Licensor name] hereby grants to [partner] a nonexclusive royalty-free, irrevocable, license to reproduce, adapt, distribute, display, perform, modify, and otherwise use the Processes.*

A complex grant statement has multiple sections. For instance, a consulting firm in the Web site development industry created a licensing and distribution partnership with a large insurance firm to create and deliver its products over the Internet. This partnership agreement necessitated several sections of licensing grants. One covered the tools and technologies owned by the consulting firm that it was licensing to the insurance firm for usage with its clients:

During the Term, [consulting firm] hereby grants to [insurance firm] a royalty-free, limited, revocable, license to reproduce, adapt, distribute, display, perform, modify, and otherwise use the Work Product [previously defined by the consulting firm in the definitions] solely as needed to perform the [product package service].

At the same time, the consulting firm was creating a new means to deliver the insurance firm's products over the Internet. Another licensing clause granted the consulting firm the ability to customize the insurance firm's products for Internet usage. It is not surprising that the stipulation required by the larger firm is fraught with additional language. It is not uncommon for the language of publicly held companies to be much more detailed than a smaller firm:

[Insurance firm] hereby grants [consulting firm] for the Term of this Agreement, a nonexclusive, nontransferable, personal, worldwide limited purpose, right, and license to use the [insurance firm materials and content] on the [insurance Web site], solely in accordance with the terms and conditions of this Agreement. [Insurance firm] further grants to [consulting firm] a nonexclusive, worldwide, nontransferable, personal license to use the [insurance firm] Marks only during the Term, on the [insurance firm] Web site in connection with the [service package offering], and as otherwise contemplated herein and solely according to the Usage Guidelines in Exhibit E and other conditions herein. [Consulting firm] shall fully and promptly correct and remedy any deficiencies in its use of the [insurance firm] Materials and [insurance firm] Marks, and/or the quality of the [insurance firm] Web site used in conjunction therewith, upon reasonable notice from [insurance firm].

A rule of thumb to use for the licensing grant is first to identify and agree on the intent of the grant. Once both parties agree on what has to be accomplished and delivered, the task of identifying all that could go wrong with the grant is considered. The party with more to lose is usually the larger of the two entities and as such, includes more ways to protect itself within the contract language.

2. *Performance Measurements*   LDAs often assign payments when specific objectives are achieved. Within the terms and conditions, it's vital

to establish the means in which objectives are met. I've included a few examples of the trickier partner objectives to measure, such as "improving customer support."

In the following example, a consumer goods manufacturer has licensed its product to a retail company, which customized the product and now sells, supports, and maintains the product. In order for the retail firm to remain as a strategic partner, it must meet customer service quality standards. The two firms mutually created the following measures of success for quality standards for customer service:

> *Evaluation and Review Services. Within thirty (30) to forty-five (45) days after the product ships, [retail firm] shall cause a [firm] Consultant to schedule and provide a consultation to the consumer. Such consultation will be to answer initial consumer questions and provide further suggestions for product placement opportunities. [Retail firm] shall also cause a [firm] Consultant to provide a marketing review to each consumer once every six (6) months for the duration of the consumer's use. Such review shall include provision of the Marketing Review Questionnaire to the consumer via the [firm] e-mail. Following a consumer's completion of such Marketing Review Questionnaire and using the Marketing Review Script, [firm] shall initiate a followup telephone conversation between the [firm] Consultant and consumer to assist the consumer in identifying additional product placement opportunities and to provide recommendations to the consumer regarding means of exploiting such opportunities.*

In this partnership, both companies desired access to the feedback in order to identify new product opportunities, even though it was the retail firm's responsibility to gather the information. The retail firm agreed to share information but determined how the data would be evaluated and reviewed. The following paragraph states the specifics:

> *At the mutual agreement of [consumer manufacturer] and the [retail firm], [firm] shall modify this marketing review process so that it may be offered to other [firm] customers and be offered on the [firm] Web site, and the Parties shall evaluate the opportunities for such offerings. In the event the Parties mutually agree upon the offering of the marketing review service in whole or in part by [firm] to other [consumer manufacturer]*

customers, the Parties shall negotiate the terms and conditions of such offering, including but not limited to the compensation to be paid to Agent, and shall enter into a written agreement memorializing such agreement.

3. *Product Performance Level*   Large companies attempt to lower the fees they will pay to a smaller company, and they will do so by attempting to cast doubt on the expected performance of the smaller firm's product lines. You can maintain your desired price by adding a performance-level standard to the LDA. If this is a new product and you have no idea how to measure product performance, place a 90-day term into the LDA. This stipulation gives you time to track customer feedback and performance of your product. It also enables you to get your asking price with a 90-day review period. If your product performs poorly, you have time to assess your options. On the other hand, if the product outperforms expectations, you have the ability to renegotiate the terms of the deal. Either way, the risk to both parties is only three months. The following paragraph was added by the retail firm to an agreement with the consumer manufacturing firm:

> **Performance Level.** *Within ninety (90) days of the [product launch], the Parties shall mutually agree upon appropriate performance measurements and evaluations of overall consumer satisfaction and appropriate reductions in the fees set forth in Section 2.2.8 (the payment schedule) for [firm's] failure to meet the agreed-upon performance levels. Upon such Agreement the Parties shall amend this Agreement in accordance with Section 10.14. Notwithstanding the foregoing, in the event the Parties fail to agree upon the performance measurement and evaluation described in this Section 2.1.8, Section 2.1.5 or Section 2.1.6(c), [consumer manufacturer] shall have the right to notify [firm] of its dissatisfaction with [firm's] performance and shall provide in writing a reasonably detailed list of deficiencies. In the event [firm] fails to cure the deficiencies within 120 days, [consumer manufacturer] shall have the right to terminate this Agreement in accordance with Section 7.2.5.*

4. *Licensing Payments*   Licensing and distribution agreements split payments into an advance paid on signing and a royalty schedule based on the projections. For each sale, the product earns a royalty on net receipt.

   For example, you don't want to pay an advance royalty if the development is being subsidized by the licensor in return for a revenue share of future products using the recipe. Instead, you will want to pay a percentage of a product earned royalty on net receipts from the products in accordance with the terms and conditions already set forth. If your LDA is structured such that you supply the finished product to a third-party network who retails it to the consumer (as opposed to your selling directly to the consumer), you will pay an earned royalty. You pay this to the licensor in the event that "you provide any portion of Work to third parties on a transaction basis."

For instance, let's say you created a cookie using the recipe licensed from Ouray Foods. You then sold your cookies to the local school system. You would be obliged to pay Ouray Foods earned royalty on a percentage of the revenue generated from this channel. The legal terminology covering this event would read as follows: "[Your firm] shall pay [Ouray Foods] Licensor a ten (10) percent royalty on Net Receipts generated directly from such transactional or packaged products." While the percentage appears high, so too are your margins. Ouray Foods as the licensor is taking advantage of the role its recipe played in making this type of transaction possible in the first place.

Within this section are terms stating payment time frames. Usually royalties are accounted for and paid within 45 days after the end of a quarterly period. Wire payments have been used for quite some time, eliminating time delays associated with manual checks. Royalty payments may be withheld if product returns are excessively high. The term *excessively high* is defined to the approval of both firms, and a *reserve* is typically created to protect you from paying royalties on returned products and suffering a cash-flow issue. In most cases, 15 percent of royalty payments are withheld from the Licensor and placed in a separate fund to protect against product returns.

5. *Guarantees* The ability to keep cash flow consistent is paramount to all businesses, particularly in a cash-starved environment stemming from economic or market pressures. The best means of ensuring that your company has the resources to keep the doors open and the lights on are guaranteed payments. Payment guarantees are important when you are licensing your product to another firm whose product sales expectations are high. They are also used when you desire to motivate your partner to promote your product to ensure success.

Most guarantee statements are one or two lines at most. Guarantees become complex when the partnership is formed on the basis of "promised projections," causing one firm to invest time and money into creating an infrastructure without producing any orders. To reduce the risk to the usually smaller firm, the larger company provides a guaranteed payment. This guarantee will stop when the consumer demand catches up and the smaller partner generates enough cash to become cash flow positive on the partner's product line.

The following example is taken from a retail firm who has partnered with a furniture manufacturer. The furniture manufacturer is well established, but it is introducing a new product line for which consumer awareness and demand are lacking. The smaller retail firm is taking advantage of the opportunity to be the "first company on the block" with the new furniture, while at the same time assuming the risk that the furniture line could be a dud.

To give incentive to the retail partner, the manufacturer included the following guarantee in the distribution agreement:

> *In the first contract year or until such time as [retail] Agent attains one thousand orders, [manufacturing firm] shall guarantee to [retail] Agent either (a) a minimum of two hundred and fifty (250) Order Acknowledgments per contract year quarter, or (b) in the event [retail] Agent fails to provide at least five hundred and fifty (550) Order Acknowledgments in any contract quarter, a payment equal to the difference between the number of Order Acknowledgments provided in such contract quarter and five hundred and fifty (550) multiplied by the fee set forth in column D of Section 2.2.8.*

Exhibits   Liberal use of exhibits will keep the LDAs as short as possible and to the point. The secret to success in using exhibits is that they must be explicit. The marketing exhibit is the most often overlooked but the most important to small companies. It's a pain to negotiate and include in an agreement, particularly if the licensor is going to be held accountable. But it is well worth it.

A few common examples of marketing stipulations provide for increased awareness and promotion. For instance, "including acknowledgment of [your firm] in all published materials" and "Licensor shall

display [your firm] logo, tagline, and acknowledgments" in all promotional activity for relevant products are reasonable requests. This is
vital if your firm is a small company licensing a key product from the
licensor. Conversely, the licensor requires "text of all marketing and
promotional materials for review" and that your firm's promotions "be
consistent with other Licensor food offers." Turnaround times such as
48 hours are included, as well as the inability of either party to withhold
approval for reasonable and consistent marketing promotions.

Global Addenda   The final licensing or distribution agreement itself
will range from 5 to 30 pages depending on its complexity. On the
bright side, using addenda shortens the agreement, increases your flexibility, and reduces your risk.

One area in which the suggestion for a "future addendum" is reasonable includes the *global addenda* by which the agreement is "modified and
amended" to extend the definitions section of the agreement. The specific definitions include global products and the specific change to the
product line to facilitate such a change. The solution offered to the market is the second added definition. This definition includes the terms of
the solution, including elements such as the status or title of distributor,
the provider of the support (if not the same), and the target market.

The second aspect of the addendum is under the distribution,
where the geographic or demographic boundaries are expanded. This
might also include a deletion of a section in the original agreement that
is rendered irrelevant or conflicting with the new agreement.

Two other components are added in a global addendum: quarterly
reporting and product or version limitations. The former is particularly
important for international expansion, which sometimes leads to price
gouging. Software manufacturer Comdisco Systems had an experience
in which it extended a licensing and distribution agreement to a firm in
a European country. After 12 months, this firm was selling one or two
products every year while firms in neighboring countries were selling
hundreds. After requesting an audit, Comdisco Systems found that the
partner was selling the software for a quarter of a million dollars per
software desktop. The suggested retail list price at the time was $50,000.
Comdisco Systems learned the hard way that it had failed to dictate
pricing parameters or establish success metrics for its partners as a basis
for agreement cancellation with cause. Immediately upon the discovery,

it modified its partner agreements, but it was forced to buy out the distribution rights from this particular partner.

Product Integration Agreements

Key to product integration agreements are the definitions, which specifically define the products "to be integrated," what it means "to integrate," and all the specific actions required for this to occur. Ownership of the existing products is identified, and the final owner of the "packaged solution" is likewise confirmed. This language is the same as the language used in the licensing definitions and grant sections. Similarly, the payments and guarantee terms and terminology are consistent to the LDAs. The primary difference between those agreements and the product integration agreement is the text relating to the intellectual property.

This is the most important facet of this agreement, and the complexity starts on one end with simple terms that prevent your removal of the partner's logo during any part of the customized solution, to ownership of new components developed during the product integration process.

Maintaining confidentiality throughout the product integration process is important to gaining an edge on the competition. Confidentiality is written into a product integration agreement through the disclosure section. This section is very long, so I've included only the most important and often overlooked clause. It has to do with covering consultants and other persons who will have contact with the product integration efforts on a need-to-know basis. Without this clause, you expose yourself to a lawsuit for unwittingly leaking information:

> *Each Party may disclose the terms and conditions of this Agreement to its employees, Affiliates, and its immediate legal and financial consultants on a need-to-know basis as required in the ordinary course of that Party's business, provided, however, that such employees, Affiliates, and legal or financial consultants are bound (or agree in writing in advance of disclosure to be bound) by confidentiality obligations at least as stringent as those imposed by the NDA. Each Party may disclose Confidential Information as required by government or judicial order, provided, however, that each Party gives each other Party prompt notice of such order before making disclosure and complies with any protective order (or equivalent) imposed on such disclosure.*

Embedded Agreements

Templates for embedded agreements are rare, even for large companies who utilize them daily for partnership agreements. This is because embedded, or OEM, agreements are largely customized. Instead of using a template for the agreement, the majority of companies who use OEM agreements instead use a background account information template. They do so to discover the intent of the potential OEM. Armed with this information, the licensor of the product will create an OEM agreement that will meet its desire to push its product into the market while meeting the objectives of the licensee.

Your account manager at the PPO will ask you to fill out an account or partner information background check sheet. If this sounds intimidating, don't worry. The questions start with the identification of the PPO products involved and the project quantities of your product intended to include the PPO's product line. It asks you to describe the "value-added solution" you intend to provide. This is very important to ascertaining its strategic importance in the industry. It is also the hinge on which the door of favorable terms will hang. Additional questions cover the target industry for the solution, the intended user, and the user demographics. This aids the PPO's determination of your target market alignment with the PPO's existing or future market concentration.

Expect the background check to include questions on international scope or intention, identification of any other agreements with the PPOs competitors, the time frame for OEM of the product, and the level of contacts your company has at the PPO's executive staff.

While this document is a one- or two-page form, don't use this as a response mechanism. Consider it a formal request for proposal and respond accordingly. Your ability to frame your value proposition to the finance team during the agreement stage is no less important than it was during the due-diligence product evaluation phase.

Marketing Agreements

Marketing agreements are written quite differently from other formal partnership agreements. Marketing agreements tend to be short and resemble a business plan as opposed to a contract. They are free of contractual language, representing information in a fill-in-the-blank format. As such, it's important you create your checklist of what the marketing agreement should contain for your own purposes.

The first section covers two main components. The first is the go-to-market coordination. This states the intent of both companies. For instance, two companies "agree to cooperate in the development, delivery, and marketing of a solution targeting the retail, financial, and manufacturing markets." This establishes that a solution will be jointly identified, created, and manufactured for specific vertical industries. It has implications for product marketing, as well as marketing communications and development groups who create, promote, and further a product in the marketplace. This statement is supported by an agreement "to specifically target enterprise customer markets which are defined as organizations with between 1000 and 5000 employees. Secondary target markets include health care and services." A very specific target audience is included, reducing the potential for miscommunication or error between the two marketing organizations. By including secondary target markets, the work done today is done with an eye toward applicability to the target markets of tomorrow.

Mutual commitments compose the next section of the document. This includes a variety of specific campaigns that will support the agreement objective. For instance, basic terms include reciprocal content on respective Web sites and Web site link rights, reciprocal logo usage rights, mutually defined success metrics and management process, and quarterly management planning and business reviews. Moderate terms include an escalation process to formally engage both firms in the event that issues appear to prevent solution delivery, establishing an escalation process to facilitate resolution of critical account sales situations in a timely manner, and reciprocal, cooperative, proactive engagement in the consulting and sales teams.

The most detailed marketing agreement commitments include co-operative marketing planning including press releases, joint marketing funds, seminars, industry conferences, client references, case studies, and a formal marketing and public relations plan. The most strategic commitment within this section is the inclusion of a partnership agreement joint board. This assigns appropriate personnel responsible for strategic direction of the relationship, evaluation of mutually agreed upon metrics and escalation of issues and opportunities. In short, it's senior-level executive visibility and sponsorship of the partnership.

The third and fourth pages include the detailed programs of how each commitment will be fulfilled. For example, *target account penetra-*

tion specifies that the first partner "shall develop a target account list with each (partner name) district at the beginning of each year and will penetrate 25 percent of the agreed upon list of targeted accounts each year during the term of the engagement." Under *geographic expansion,* the same company "shall, in cooperation with (partner name) identify, open, and staff a minimum of (number) new office locations each year during the term of the agreement."

The most important facet in many marketing agreements is the promotion of the customer success stories. No marketing program is as effective as a testimonial from a happy customer. This promotion is managed by a section covering wins, references, and case studies. Identified within this section are the *wins, internal and external references,* and *case studies* to be delivered in specific time periods for the duration of the agreement. This ensures that a minimum number of tools are released to the market every calendar period.

Perhaps second in importance for small companies is the *marketing spend* term. This term identifies that each company "will allocate and spend a minimum of $*XX* annually during the term of the agreement toward marketing and go-to-market objectives." This may or may not include the total company investment in the partnership.

The last page of the agreement includes the direct funding from one company to another (usually the larger to the smaller) and the distribution of funds by quarter. Generally recognized categories include acquisition costs (this relates specifically to customer acquisition costs associated with lead generation), expansion/accelerated hiring/workshop content, general marketing, and consulting. The *total direct funding* of the marketing partnership is then totaled. The payout, or *distribution of funds,* is below the total.

This page ends with identifying how the marketing agreement will be funded. Some companies account for the marketing agreement funds as a "loan until programs are executed." This is done most often when a large company wires the funds to the smaller company, with the small company responsible for delivering the programs. When completed, the "loan" is forgiven. Payments can be made quarterly from different marketing, product, or operations budgets as a straight cost. The most important points to place in the contract are the instruments, conversion, governance, confidentiality, contingency, and nonbinding effects of the agreement. With these terms included, you will know your obligations, rights, and certainty of the power of the marketing agreement. It will also be a proof point of the impact the marketing agreement is expected to have on your firm.

Master Agreements

The intent behind a master agreement is to identify where partners complement, overlap, and compete. It is then used as a basis for all communication to customers, prospects, sales and marketing personnel, and even the press. A master agreement virtually eliminates the risk of negativity from either company toward the other or conflicts in the customer base. This creates the impression (which is reality in most cases) that the two firms are completely unified on a core level (Table 8–2).

The first task is to define the overlap and what percentage of product overlap exists, then agree to be "above board" about where they compete so it won't "spoil the pie," said Kris Hagerman of VERITAS Software, who is very familiar with master agreements. In areas of greater overlap, you set up general rules of engagement for competition—"segmenting into buckets where we fight and where we are on the same side such as relying on the partner's distribution engine and so forth," explained Hagerman. "By identifying the buckets and placing products into those buckets, we can take advantage and grow much quicker than if we didn't talk to one another." Overlapping and fully competitive situations require the partners to establish the messages, data points, and sales tools so the internal and external teams are unified, or at least don't cross marketing hairs with one another.

No doubt this provides a certain visibility to the future product lines of the partner. But this is all balanced with a willingness to be creative and pragmatic. "It's hard to be directly competitive and religious at the same time, so the issue is how to structure the agreement where we don't force that partner to damage something that is critically important to him or her," Hagerman adds. That's the kind of pro-partner attitude that should be adopted by more companies.

Considerations, Hold-Backs, and Double Hold-Backs

Any agreement that specifies payment is liable to include one or three phrases whose use to this point has been limited only to partnerships including investments. These are *consideration, hold-backs,* and *double hold-backs.* While terms on payments and guarantees are inherently

Table 8–2 Master Agreement Matrix

	Complement	Overlap	Compete
Product sets: Company A and Company B listed.	Markets, sales types, etc., named.	Markets, sales types, etc. named.	Markets, sales types, etc. named.
Product positioning statements supported by evidence points.	Positive.	Neutral and customer oriented.	Outline the strengths for particular markets and customer usage situations.
Evidence points.	Joint customer wins where the teams worked together from start to finish.	Where each product's strength served the customer for two situations: one where both were chosen to complement one another despite the overlap, and two, where one chosen was picked over the other, why, and how these situations can be identified early in the sales cycle.	The customer requirements and profiles. Where the territories, markets, and customer segmentation start and end. This might include passing outright competitive situations to partners to handle.
Process.	When and how the companies will share; who will support the customer.	When and how they will work together; defer to one another or pass the prospect situation to a partner.	What is said, when, and how to the potential customer by each organization or by the partner.
Marketing.	Determined at both the field and corporate level.	Determined at the corporate level but some flexibility given to the local offices.	Determined and mandated by the corporate organization.
Conflict resolution.	If it arises, handled at the local level.	When arises, handled at local level first with corporate awareness if serious.	Handled at local level but made visible to corporate immediately. Guidance by corporate almost always a requirement.

straightforward and relatively simple, even the most knowledgeable alliance manager can be stumped when any of these terms is thrown into an agreement.

The consideration describes the initial amount to be paid to one partner at the start of the agreement. It could be the first payment on a guarantee or the up-front payment on a joint marketing agreement, investment, joint development agreement, or even acquisition. For example:

> *Consideration.* *In consideration for the [agreement type], [payor] will pay [your firm] one million dollars, ($1,000,000) (the "Consideration").*

The hold-back is the portion of the payment associated with an agreement that will be held back for some reason. This is used any time the firm paying the money believes it is at risk of employees leaving the company, the product delivery schedule being upheld, or any other unforeseen and unpreventable event. You are wise to employ the hold-back if you are faced with this situation.

The same contract would continue with the hold-back clause:

> *Hold-back.* *($750,000) Seventy-five percent (75 percent) of that portion of the Consideration (the "Restricted Amount") otherwise payable to [your firm] at the [agreement] Closing shall be paid out (75 percent up front) remaining paid out over two years, in equal installments over four years, with 25 percent of the Restricted Amount payable at each of the first, second, third, and fourth anniversaries of the Closing.*

The double hold-back is the amount held back on the total amount for the duration of the agreement. This is another insurance policy for the partner with the most risk. Be sure to look at the paragraph carefully, as I've never seen an agreement that calls out a double hold-back within the main hold-back paragraph:

> *Twenty percent (20 percent) of the Consideration will be withheld following the Closing (the "Hold-back"). [Payor] will be entitled to be indemnified from the Hold-back in the event of a breach by [your firm] or its Principals of any of their respective representations and warranties, or a failure to comply with any of the covenants, in the Definitive Agreement(s), provided that [Payor's] right to indemnification shall not be limited to the amount of the Hold-back.*

Deal Term Inversion

The prevalent use of double hold-backs and other fun terms is the product of the bursting dot.com bubble and flighty millionaires. I've no qualm laying the blame of this at the feet of those who made out well financially after the closure of an agreement and elected not to stay

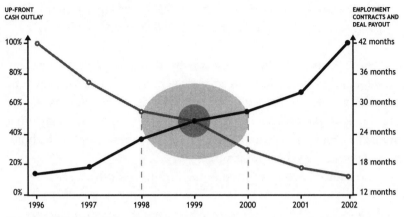

Figure 8–1 Deal Term Inversion

to fulfill product, marketing, or sales commitments. As "opportunity cost ran high" according to one such CEO, it was well worth it to leave a company high and dry after just a few months to start another venture.

As the trend of executive management team turnover heightened (for it wasn't just the CEO who jumped ship), favorable deal terms started to disappear. I refer to this as a *deal term inversion* (Figure 8–1). Individuals regularly involved in the creation of partner agreements clearly saw the trends that started well before the economic downturn.

Before 2001, these terms were little known among even the most savvy corporate development groups. In fact, I was dealing with a former vice president of Wells Fargo finance and acquisitions who had made the jump to a large software company. He wasn't even familiar with the term *hold-back*, let alone *double hold-back*. At the same time, industry monolith Microsoft had been pioneering creative ways to use double hold-backs, which confused a great many prospective partners.

In 2000 I sold a company that received 68 percent of the consideration within the first year and the remainder within 24 months. Another company in 2001 was purchased with over 50 percent consideration given and a hold-back of only one and a half years. However, in both cases, what made those agreements work was tying payouts to key product deliverables and projecting revenue payback within that time frame. As such, the risk of payback was therefore considered relatively low. Sobered entrepreneurs and CEOs are now more realistic when approaching the negotiation table.

Partnership Break Fees

In any of the above agreements, the line from an informal to a formal agreement is crossed when penalties are assigned for failure to reach a final agreement. For instance, if a company desires to be acquired and attains a letter of intent from an acquisition suitor, a term is placed within the LOI identifying a fee due to the acquiree should the acquirer fail to meet the stated deadlines or step away from the deal. Depending on the risk, market environment, and size of the deal, the penalty can range up to 7 percent of the deal, or be assessed as fees from several thousands to millions of dollars.

Generally speaking, deal break fees are assigned by the type of partnership agreement. Licensing and distribution break fees are usually determined to be worth 3 to 12 months' worth of estimated royalties. Joint development break fees range from 7 to 12 percent of the total value of the development project. In both situations, the fee is large enough to cover lost sales due to a potentially profitable partnership with another firm. Marketing break fees cover up-front program costs or are amortized over the course of the intended campaign. This is usually invoked only when the program has been halted for some reason.

Acquisitions and investment break fees are based upon the opportunity cost associated with market conditions. This set figure is augmented with a percentage of the *estimated* final acquisition price. In one instance, the break fee was established at $300,000, or 3 percent of the estimated deal value of $10 million. This deal break fee stood unchanged even though the deal was ultimately closed at $8 million. One had little bearing on the ultimate outcome of the other.

The Art of Contractual Negotiations

Since creating an alliance is the result of many months of work that goes on at many levels of complexity, the sales negotiation tactic of coming in hard for the close doesn't usually work when refining the contract. To get what you want in your agreement, you will have to be doing the right thing every step of the way. If you have done your homework, set the correct foundation with the business case, conducted a proper due-diligence review, and set expectations the entire way with the PPO, the negotiations are a piece of cake. A few techniques are often used to keep the price high and to understand how your firm is going to be evaluated during an acquisition negotiation.

The Mistake of Bringing Up Legacy Information

During an acquisition pitch, the biggest mistake sellers make is bringing up the history of a product. Acquiring companies want to be reassured that the product is innovative and fresh. The PPO's bubble is burst when it is told a product was "not so great in its first iteration, and because of a change in management, it had a second iteration so this version is really top notch," as one software engineer unwisely disclosed to the financial manager of the potential acquiring firm.

Keep the details invisible and coach your people to do the same. After the company has been acquired, you are free to have hallway conversation over coffee about the real history of your product line. But until that happens, keep your mouth shut.

Determining a Price

The 1 percent of high-flying, multi-million-dollar acquisitions based on market projections or hype has largely gone nowhere. In direct contrast are the most modest acquisitions that are steadily producing revenue streams. The majority of these acquisition offers were based on thorough financial modeling conducted by product and finance departments.

Corporate development groups have formulas to estimate the value of potential acquisitions. While the models vary from company to company, three criteria are always considered. These are cost of integration, cost of assimilation, and cost of innovation. Simply stated, the cost of each to the acquiring organization is estimated during the negotiation process and deducted from the acquisition offer. This is one of the reasons acquisitions offers are regularly one tenth of the estimated value. It is important for the outside company approaching a PPO to understand what each item means and how it can anticipate the argument in a way to limit its impact on the final acquisition price.

Cost of Integration Integrating product lines of two companies is never easy. It is the job of the finance group to determine the cost of integration prior to making an acquisition proposal. The number of staff work hours, capital costs, and other investments will be tabulated. The final cost is then deducted from the acquisition offer.

One way you can reduce the size of the deduction is to provide evidence of past product integration efforts. If this is not available, you need to create a road map for the integration of the products accompanied by an associated budget. You should strip out every cost that can be assumed and accomplished by your organization prior to the acquisition. Provide this information to the corporate development department to use as a baseline of past performance. Doing so is much better than waiting for the analysts at the acquiring firm to use worst-case performance models.

The finance group will build in another line-item cost for "marketing integration costs." This refers to the cost of positioning the new company and product line—that is, the cost of changing logos, branding, marketing materials, sales materials, and the like.

The best thing you can do is anticipate these two integration factors and build baseline estimates into your acquisition proposal. This requires that you work with your peer manager from the acquiring firm to ascertain realistic uses of the product once the company has been acquired. If you can do a reasonable job, the finance group will rein in how broadly they calculate marketing, sales, support, and other costly infrastructure costs associated with the acquisition.

Cost of Assimilation   The first aspect measured by the corporate development team is the cost of integrating your product into their product line. The second is the cost associated with the assimilation of your organization into the acquiring firm.

Companies usually factor in *dead time* before a new team can be productive. While you move and are assigned a role, a functioning computer, and a phone line, you are considered a cost center, not a profit center. The finance group will be concerned with providing immediate revenue return. It is your job to show that the team being acquired can produce a return in less than three months.

Support this argument by showing your team's understanding of the partner's product line, culture, processes, and functioning departments. It is likely that you are very knowledgeable about these tactical aspects anyway since the acquisition might be due to a prior working relationship that has graduated to an acquisition. Aid this argument by showing examples of your team successfully working with various departments within the acquiring firm.

Cost of Innovation   Once the price tag for the integration of existing products and assimilation of personnel is tabulated, the final deduction to the acquisition offer will be calculated. This is the cost for maintaining your product line over a period of three years.

Finance teams use a simple model to determine the costs behind this factor. It is the combination of the existing team product and/or engineering teams raised by an additional 30 percent head count year over year for three years. Standard support costs from marketing, operations, and other relevant groups are added as well.

It is this facet of the acquisition modeling that poses the greatest threat to your firm. First, it is hard to realistically anticipate how your product will be supported over such a long period of time. For all you know, the product might be wiped out within 12 months. The acquiring company doesn't have to guarantee continuance of the product line, and such clauses are very rare in acquisition agreements. Furthermore, the costs associated with supporting product lines change dramatically with operational efficiencies. The acquiring company might be using the numbers from the least profitable or efficient business unit instead of the most profitable group.

The best strategy to remove hidden costs such as are found in the cost of innovation is to proactively provide your own estimates of supporting the product line over the first three years. In reality, you will have already been asked to provide this during the technical and financial due-diligence reviews. Armed with your own product and financial plans, it is a matter of mutually determining how the costs of innovation will actually decrease through the use of the acquiring firm's organizational capabilities.

When Agreements Define Partnerships

The worst-case scenario is when you have negotiated an agreement and you are unhappy with the result. Mike Walsh is a veteran at creating partnerships. After graduating from Stanford, he worked his way up the ranks at Visa International, Comdisco Systems, and Navigation Technologies, each time raising the firm to new levels of revenue and market leadership through the use of smart partnerships. With each new venture there were cultural, economic, and philosophical barriers to creating a partnership, yet in each situation, he found a way to adapt the best aspects of partnerships to the needs of his company. Now as the CEO of Actify Corporation, he describes the most damaging aspect of creating a partnership, what I call the *inverted agreement definition*. Instead of a partnership defining the agreement, the agreement defines the partnership.

"The agreement just puts into words what you have been working on for the entire time," describes Walsh. "Yet somehow, with each participant's trying to make sure its agendas are being met, the agreement puts an entirely different face on the original partnership." Having seen this as an active participant as well as on the sidelines as a board member, Walsh believes this to be the highest risk aspect of the entire partnership. "If you haven't come to terms on the intent of the partnership well before this time, the agreement creation process will destroy the partnership before it ever starts."

CHAPTER

9

The Tools Used
to Create Partnerships

CHAPTER HIGHLIGHTS

- *Eleven tools used in all partnership development creation cycles*
- *The five-letter acronym that guarantees a return phone call*
- *The single biggest accelerator for partnership development*

WHEN THE BASQUES sought to create a partnership, they used an epistle, note, letter, or other recognized written form to convey their business case to the potential partner. Their handwritten proposals were composed on parchment and leather. In modern times we deliver our business case through e-mail or through a *PowerPoint* presentation. The intent then as now is to achieve a specific partnership development objective.

Unlike the pioneering Basques, we have more flexibility in adapting our method of communication to the culture of our potential partner. The written word is often complemented by checklists, conference calls and product demonstrations. All these items can be considered *tools* with which you can present your point of view to the partner. This chapter will cover each tool intended to educate and convince prospective partners of the value to be had in a partnership with your firm.

Alliance Managers and the Pitch

It's safe to say that most partner alliance practitioners view "pitching the company" as singularly the most challenging part of the job. It doesn't take a rocket scientist to get on the phone and promote a company through a 10-second pitch. It's just that cold-calling is a skill set usually perceived as the exclusive domain of telemarketers, public relations professionals, and the sales executives.

Ironically, alliance managers have much in common with these professionals. Each must provide a convincing value proposition within 10 seconds. Each represents products, companies, or personalities to skeptical and sometimes antagonistic recipients. Getting stonewalled is common. Rejection is expected. The very best professionals in each industry are tenacious, aggressive, and skilled in adapting essentially the same story for different audiences. They are also able to assist in creating a story, product package, or solution that fits the needs of their listener.

Alliance managers likewise pitch to many individuals within the potential partner organizations. This never-ending cycle starts with a business decision maker, progresses to the product group, the engineering group, then back to the business group, and ultimately, with the finance corporate development group. At each turn of the corner, the pitch is tailored to the agenda of that decision maker. And with every change, the format of that pitch might also change.

Leveraged Tools

Just as scripts aid telemarketers and sale representatives in closing a sell, alliance managers create all manner of tools to use again and again for their pitch. With minor changes, these tools can then be used with other partners. The tools are also used by others on your team who need to communicate the positioning, messages, or benefits associated with a particular partner strategy.

If you have a tool set already, read this chapter with an eye to filling in pieces that you may have overlooked. If you are just starting your efforts, identify the tools relevant to where you are now so you can start setting aside time to build the pieces for when you need them. I've included a snapshot of tools used in the partnership development process that can serve as a guideline for your own efforts (Table 9–1).

Table 9–1   Tool Matrix

Tool	When Used	Strategic or Tactical	Audience
Partner database	All the time	Both	Internal team
Mini-value proposition	Phase I	Both, 70/30	Business decision maker
Voice mail message	Phase I	Tactical	Business decision maker
E-mail message	Phase I	Both, 90/10	Business decision maker
Interim presentation	Phase I	Both, 80/20	Business decision maker
Premeeting brief	All phases	Both, 30/70	Internal team
Phase I presentation	Phase I	Both, 80/20	Business decision maker(s); product teams with potentially others attending
Extended value proposition	Phase 2	80/20	Business, technical, and product decision makers
Product presentation	Phase 2	90/10	Technical and product groups
Interim proposal	Phase 2	90/10	Business decision maker
Proposal presentation	Phase 2	80/20	Technical and product groups
Final presentation	Phase 2	70/30	Technical, product, and business groups

Partnership Database

The first step to leveraged sales efforts is to place contact names, information, and relevant customer facts in a central location. Alliance managers should do the same. You may have no idea how many other people within your organization could benefit from having access to what you have created or know about potential partnerships.

Our computer server has a folder for each organization with whom we have created a partnership. Within this folder are the tools that produce the most successful outcome for each type of partnership. This includes value propositions, presentations, premeeting briefs, e-mails, and even the verbal pitches created for the targeted decision maker.

The framework we created is segmented into the partnership development life cycle. Consider, for example, the partnership development phase 1 and the tools for verbal pitches. Within this folder are 10-, 30-, and 60-second pitches for the business manager, product manager, program manager, technical evangelist, and senior manager. When pitching a client to a particular organization, we access the master file for the organization, pick out the decision-maker role targeted, review our catalog of recommended pitches, and then select the most appropriate pitch.

Replacing the Rolodex

Remember that one of the primary reasons it takes three to six months to craft an alliance is personnel turnover. While this is primarily at the potential partner organization, it also occurs within your own company. Getting information into a database removes the uncertainty and doubt associated with the Rolodex factor and dependence on a single individual.

As this occurs within your organization, don't settle for simple contact information. Build the organizational chart surrounding the contact. While we were working on a partnership with the Sony Corporation, we built an entire organizational map that links Sony and its affiliates through its network of investments, partnerships, joint ventures, and just about everything in between. In this way, we can quickly understand if any entity related to Sony has an existing partnership that may compete or be complementary with a client in seconds.

This management of information may sound overwhelming for a small company, but it's not. We started with Microsoft *Excel* and then after a few years upgraded to SQL. The initial cost was not even calculated (a few hours of time). Later, as we customized some aspects to provide visual representations of all the intricacies peculiar to our firm, the cost did increase. Yet this was neither challenging to our limited resources (we outsourced it), time-consuming (several weeks), nor expensive (less than $50,000). For a growing firm, simple database tracking is a must-have.

Phase I   Partnership Development Tools:
The Mini-Value Proposition

Next to the database, the major time investment is creating the right documents. Developing a high-impact value proposition can easily consume a few hours. To limit the time you give to unnecessary documents, start with the most essential pieces, and graduate to larger documents as desired by the PPO.

The first document of this nature is the *mini-value proposition*. The mini-value proposition is an introductory document that is presented to the potential partnering organization to determine potential partner fit. It is a brief synopsis of your company, product, and the business opportunity. It has five components that provide the key aspects for the partnerships. The intent of the document is to get the decision maker at the PPO on the phone. This piece is leveraged when it is used as a follow-up tool to be sent to educate others internally and externally about the goals for a partnership. It is also leveraged when used as the guidepost for the interim conference call during phase 1.

The first section is the executive overview. This section presents the high-level overview of your firm, the primary product under discussion, and its market focus and primary product functions. It is written to summarize the business opportunity, technical alignment, and company history.

One company approaching American Express wrote the following preface:

> *The essence of the proposed relationship between The American Express Company and (our firm) is to add value, without up-front cost, to the wide range of core products and services currently being marketed on- and offline by American Express Travel, Corporate Services, Card Accounts, Travelers Cheques, (other stored-value instruments), and American Express Membership Rewards.*

Below this preface were two paragraphs of detail that completed the executive overview. In short, it identified the product line, partnership positioning, potential revenue, partnership required, and dependencies in a concise and easy-to-read manner.

The business opportunity is the second section. It represents the win-win scenario for both your firm and the potential partner. It also provides detail on the targeted market segment, identifying growth areas and highlighting the potential advantages the client can offer the partner in this market area—that is, barriers to competition. Each section should not be longer than one paragraph.

One firm who created a distribution partnership for its insurance services used the following business opportunity case in the mini-value proposition:

The individual and small-business market segments represent the largest, fastest-growing, and most profitable market in the insurance provider business, in excess of $350 billion. Our firm would like to partner with [partner] to create an interactive online resource through which: (1) Consumers can access information and education on insurance carriers via the [name portal] [a resource center thus, recurring eyes]. (2) [Partner] can act as an online insurance brokerage for those consumers. And (3) [partner] can provide an e-commerce distribution solution for insurance carriers seeking revenue and a greater market share of the individual and small-business segment.

Currently, the revenue commission on small-group and individual insurance policies is approximately 10 percent, from which [our firm] estimates the traditional distribution opportunity to be approximately $10 to $15 billion. This commission revenue is now paid to the over 225,000 licensed brokers and agents. The online insurance distribution and enrollment market will grow from about 1 percent in 1999 to over 11 percent in 2003. By partnering with [our firm], [partner] could become a major player in this emerging market and gain significant revenue by providing the brokerage service online. [Our firm] estimates that with an approximate 18 percent market share, [partner] could achieve $226 million in revenues in 2003.

The third section is your company overview. This portion is straightforward and useful as a tool to highlight potential client advantages (that is, percentage market ownership with your product, only company to offer said service and/or product). It is a brief capsule of the company history and its strengths. The concluding section contains the next steps and rollout wherein the path for progressing the partnership is articulated.

Companies vary the last two sections depending on their culture and attitudes toward taking an aggressive next-steps approach as opposed to one that is more passive. An *active approach* is one in which a list of next steps is identified versus a simple sentence requesting an in-person meeting at the potential partner location.

Active Approach

[Our firm] offers American Express the ability to achieve eight vital objectives for growth:

1. *Secure a new service offering for its existing client base, which provides a unique, defendable, and sustainable advantage over the competition. This advantage will increase over time as [our firm] and American Express work together to develop and implement additional services.*
2. *Establish new distribution for American Express travel content, applications, and services to other members.*
3. *Provide innovative value-added benefits to American Express Merchants.*
4. *Be the source of the same service for a new customer base provided through the associations.*
5. *Deliver a net-new revenue channel with minimal investment risk or system downtime.*
6. *Generate incremental revenue through additional service offerings that can be adapted to the changing nature of traveler needs, tools, or geographic locations.*
7. *Generate additional revenues through [our firm's] clearing all its credit card transactions though an American Express financial clearing service.*
8. *Through a strategic partnership, the potential for an investment in [our firm] is a possibility.*

Passive Approach for the Same Company

[Our firm] proposes a first meeting in mid-April at the American Express Company headquarters. At that time, the detailed business case will be presented.

Tips on the Value Proposition Document

Never send a generic company overview document. Alan Bird, a director of partnership development at IBM, has thrown away "more pitches than he can count" because they were no more than cut-and-paste brochures. This provides no value at all to the reader and shows that you haven't thought long and hard about what a relationship will provide. Usually it just serves to irritate your prospective decision maker.

Don't ever make the value proposition longer than two pages. If you can't create a document that is enticing enough to get the right person on the phone in a page and a half, the document isn't good anyway.

According to Steve Murchie, business manager for the billion-dollar Microsoft SQL Server business unit, you "keep reworking it until it is hard hitting and relevant to the reader."

It's important to walk the line between confidence and arrogance. In the fall of 1999, a vice president at IBM received a letter from the CEO of a west coast–based software firm. The letter was sent via Federal Express, addressed to him personally, and was marked "confidential." These were smart approaches since it bypassed the administrators. Yet the tenor of the letter "all but guaranteed it went straight to the garbage," said the IBM vice president. The way in which the CEO stated that his company's products were superior to IBM's products was phrased "to the point of being obnoxious." The vice president didn't disagree that some of the points might have been accurate, but the letter conveyed the personality and culture of the interested company much more than the product. Based on that singular impression, the vice president avoided the entire discussion by throwing the letter in the trash without even bothering to send an acknowledgment via e-mail.

The Pitch: What's in It for Me

When you have navigated through the organization to find a logical entry point, you have to use a pitch. If you sent an e-mail or have left a voice mail with your pitch and haven't received a return phone call, it might be for one of the following reasons:

- "It sounded interesting, but he didn't identify what his role would be in driving the relationship."—Director at IBM
- "When I listened to the first voice mail, it sounded like it would be too much work for the payback."—Marketing manager for Sony
- "The e-mail was something like four pages. It was a novel. It needed to be two paragraphs."—Product manager at Microsoft
- "[The e-mail] had all these requirements of what we needed to do to partner with them! And I'd never even heard of them before."—Business manager at MSNBC
- "The voice mail said that it was so important that the CEO would like to fly up and meet with me in the next few days. Like I'm going to meet with anyone just because the title is a CEO."—Vice president at American Express

Clearly all of these pitches lacked something major. Essentially, it all comes down to the intent of the communiqué in the first place. The listener or reader must have a sense of how his or her firm (and perhaps he or she personally) will benefit by responding to your solicitation. This is the hook. Without the hook, the exercise will be one of frustration and futility.

A successful pitch is all about anticipating the ultimate question: What's in it for me (WIIFM)? Not what's in it for you, but what's in it for the target decision maker either personally (help me increase the sales of my organization) or for the decision maker's corporation (help me penetrate a new market).

The 10-Second Pitch

The most productive voice mail is a 10-second pitch. Anything longer than this can be hard for the receiver to retain. With only 10 seconds to work with, it is important to simplify the message into the core elements, leaving everything else for the in-person dialogue. Remember, the ultimate goal of the voice-mail pitch is a call back.

The structure of the voice mail is identical to the value proposition. It is only shorter. As in the following examples, you can employ the verbal pitch when you have completed the planning process and are armed with lots of information, but you can use this approach equally well even if you have very little:

Scenario 1: Lots of Details

Who you are, the firm you represent:
   Hi, I'm Jane Smith, director of alliances for Sonic Engineering.
Reason for the call:
   We have spoken with your top five customers, and each of them would like to place an order for our new product line.
What your firm provides, relevance to the potential partner, monetary return, and urgency:
   We develop a line of lasers to remove scarring in burn victims, and we have focused on the manufacturing industry, specifically petrochemical. The dollar value for these sales is over $1 million. We'd like to discuss a potential partnership with your firm to distribute our products, since you have an established distribution channel and our line of products could be a new line to your customers.

Call to action:

I'd like to talk with you or the appropriate business manager responsible for the product distribution decisions at your earliest convenience. I can be best reached at (number), but I will send you a follow-up informational e-mail with more details if you send me your information to (your e-mail here).

The preceding dialogue takes about 10 to 15 seconds, depending on your pace. Beyond being concise and packed with enticing information, your own version needs to reflect some amount of your personality or inflections.

This is a great introduction, you may say, but you haven't talked with the potential partner's customers (no time), and you don't have a million dollars in possible orders waiting in the wings. What you have is a good product, a good idea for a partnership, but very little else. Can you still expect a return phone call? You bet. Here is a modified version of the above that will still get a call back.

Scenario 2: Few Details

Who you are, the firm you represent:

Hi, I'm Jane Smith, director of alliances for Sonic Engineering.

Reason for the call:

I'd like to take five minutes of your time to discuss a possible partnership.

What your firm provides, relevance to the potential partner,
   monetary return, and urgency:

Our firm develops a line of lasers to remove scarring in burn victims, and we have focused on the manufacturing industry, specifically petrochemical. Based on your existing product set, our line would be a natural addition for our mutual target market, and it would require very little uptime to get going. Margins on our product are very high, and customer support requirements are negligible. We have a product launch (or promotion) coming up within (state months here), and we would like to start talks at your earliest convenience.

Call to action:

I'd like to talk with you or the appropriate business manager responsible for the product distribution decisions at your earliest con-

venience. I can be best reached at (number), but I will send you a follow-up e-mail with more details if you send me your e-mail address.

The E-Mail Pitch

Following up the voice mail should be an e-mail pitch that covers the same information in a slightly different way. As with the mini-value proposition and voice mail, the goal of this vehicle is to gain a response indicating a desire to talk about the potential partnership. Don't take this as a green light to add a lot more information; just keep it simple.

Scenario 1: Lots of Details

[Name:] As a follow-up to the voice mail that I left earlier today, I'm the business manager for Sonic Engineering. Sonic creates lasers to remove scarring in burn victims, and we have just started to focus on the petrochemical industry. I'm writing this e-mail to you in order to determine the opportunity to create a distribution partnership with your organization. I'll briefly summarize the potential.

Our three-year-old firm is now the recognized leader of lasers for treating burn victims in two other industries. We've identified petrochemical as our next target market, and we have contacted five potential customers that identified your organization as the distribution firm that they use. Each firm would like to purchase our new laser products as soon as they are available on the market. Sonic has the option to sell direcly to these firms or create a partnership with your firm so that the customer can maintain a single-source distribution house.

The benefit to you is diversification of product line, high margins (60 percent on hard goods), and customer control. The value to us is accelerated time to market without having to create an infrastructure, thus keeping our costs low and margins to distributors high.

Given this initial customer feedback and demand, I'd like to speak with you at your earliest convenience. I'll send you additional documents outlining the partnership opportunity once you confirm your role as the appropriate contact.

Thank you for your timely consideration,
Name and company.

Scenario 2: Few Details

If you lack strong data points such as customer requirements, substitute this section for the logic that supports a partnership as you did in the voice mail.

> *[Name:] As a follow-up to the voice mail that I left earlier today, I'm the business manager for Sonic Engineering. Sonic creates lasers for treating burn victims, and we have just started to focus on the petro-chemical industry. I'm writing this e-mail to you in order to determine the opportunity to create a distribution partnership with your organization. I'll briefly summarize the potential.*
>
> *Our three-year-old organization is a provider of lasers for treating burn victims. We've identified petrochemical as our next target market, and we know your organization as one that serves this market and does not have a laser in the existing product line. Sonic has the option to sell directly to this market or create a partnership with your firm so that the customer can maintain a single-source distribution house.*
>
> *If you will consider diversification in an area that will deliver high margins (60 percent on hard goods), we have the opportunity to be the first group to come to market with a solution for this area. This will accelerate our own time to market dramatically, which will keep our costs low and margins to distributors high.*
>
> *We have an upcoming product promotion through which we could promote the partnership, particularly if it is for our initial distributor. I'll send you additional documents outlining the partnership opportunity once you confirm your role as the appropriate contact.*
>
> *Thank you for your timely consideration,*
> *Name and company.*

Tips for Pitching the Potential Partner

What happens if you start to leave a voice message and someone picks up? Or worse, if your call doesn't go to voice mail at all and you get someone live. Now you have to act fast and get out of the rehearsing mode. This is the time to give additional information as well as get information absolutely critical to your partnership development needs.

If you do get someone on the phone, don't hang up before you obtain partnership-specific information. Get this *after* you make your pitch but prior to finishing the call. The person you speak to in this circumstance can actually give you substantive material that can satisfy you (and your boss) that you are on the right path. Collect information regarding the preferred partnership development process, the type of partnerships usually created, typical dependencies based on different types of alliances, realistic time frames, and upcoming strategic initiatives or deadlines that might pertain to the partnership at hand.

Interim Presentation Phase I

Once the first business manager you approach is convinced of the merits of a partnership, the two of you will set up a meeting. The goal of the meeting is to gain consensus on a unified level of interest in a partnership and agreement on the next steps for both firms. Secondarily, you can use the meeting to strengthen the position of your alliance contact in advocating for the partnership you are proposing. As this person adopts the potential partnership into his or her own agenda, he or she will start to champion your "case" to others within the organization.

The best technique to ingratiate yourself is to protect your champion from looking ill-prepared or, worse, incompetent. Set him or her up for success by giving him or her the chance to see ahead of time what you will be presenting. This will enable your champion to validate that you are meeting his or her objectives and are covering all the right hot spots of his or her organization. It then gives him or her the chance to provide feedback to you that might aid you in giving a presentation of high quality and high impact.

The key to success in this relationship is focusing on your contact. It's all about adding value every step of the way. My mantra for partnership development success is simple. If you aren't adding value to your contact with each e-mail, every phone message, and every meeting, then don't expect a call back or a good reception. This has to be ingrained in everything an alliance manager does with every interaction with the potential partner. By looking out for him or her—*he or she* will naturally start to look out for *you*.

The *interim presentation* needs to include the essence of what you will say during the first business meeting. In terms of a flow, the best model covers the five elements consistent with all the previous tools. The difference is that this presentation includes much more detail.

The first presentation should be timed to take no more than 45 minutes, which allows for a 15-minute question-and-answer session.

Scheduling any more time than an hour for a first meeting causes many individuals to decline the meeting invitation. This is simple time economics and opportunity cost. Who wants to be scheduled for over 60 minutes with a firm that no one has met with before? No one. Don't make the mistake of asking for more time. If people are interested, they will stay on their own accord.

Second, strive for a substantive meeting that takes the place of three normal initial business meetings. Completing the interim presentation as a conference call with your business contact is the best way to ensure that this occurs.

Using the five points previously discussed as your framework, the final *PowerPoint* presentation should be about 22 slides long. This number provides roughly two minutes per slide.

Tips for the Interim Presentation

Think about the one or two slides that are going to be included for your contact's review under each section.

1. Business opportunity
   a. What kind of alliance is desired (global distribution and marketing)
   b. The business justification: Units to be moved based on their estimated customers, percentage of existing customer sales, maintenance and service contracts, start-up costs, all played out over a three-year period
   c. Impact on business and market share for both partners
2. Product details
   a. What it does, how it works, and how it is relevant to the customer
   b. Unique features and competitive advantage
3. Product alignment
   a. How the product is aligned with potential partner's product set (competitive and/or complementary)
   b. Product demonstration
   c. Opportunities for new product development (to show vision and long-term focus)
4. Partnership details
   a. The framework for a relationship
   b. Key terms and desires
   c. What will be provided to the PPO in return

5. Next steps
   a. When an announcement is desired
   b. When and how sales will be ramped up
   c. Other existing activities to be included

A good alliance manager should facilitate the interim meeting by bringing in the main person that will be delivering the business case if it will not be the alliance manager himself or herself. This will ensure that a direct relationship will be started between the business manager and another person on the PPO's internal team. In the interest of saving time and money, PPOs will elect a conference call for an interim meeting if given the choice. Push for an in-person meeting.

The value of prior one-to-one introductions between the members of the two negotiating teams will be evident when everyone meets for the first time and someone other than the alliance manager has already met the business manager. A greeting that includes "It's nice to see you again" implies a relationship that has been around for a while and sets a comfort level for everyone in the room, much more so than a stiff "nice to meet you." Partnership development is as much about setting the stage for a good open conversation as it is about hard-core business.

Since it is unlikely that the interim presentation is going to be reviewed page by page, hone in on the aspects most critical to meeting the objectives. For instance, are the numbers in the first section going to be significant enough to get everyone motivated? Does the product section clearly describe how the two products fit together? Is the path for progression missing any required pieces that must be in place prior to moving into the technical due-diligence phase (such as certification)? Anything that does need to be addressed should be handled before the in-person meeting. And the completion of these items should be reported to the business manager so that he or she can be at ease that all of these concerns, at least, have been satisfied.

Clearly, there is quite a bit of work to do even before the first meeting, but these early efforts will be worthwhile in the long run. The business manager's increased confidence might give him or her the ammunition to rope all the right people into the meeting that might not otherwise have attended. Understanding more about the product aspect might enable the business manager to accelerate movement into the phase 2 activities (the first technical meeting) by bringing in one or two product or engineering decision makers. In the end, having an interim presentation review is the single biggest accelerator for partnership development in the first phase because so many individuals have the opportunity to be educated on the developing partnership. This has the result of splintering the efforts in multiple groups very quickly once the yes has been given to proceed with the relationship.

Extended Value Proposition

After the interim meeting has occurred, the business manager is likely to request something that he or she can send to others within the organization that will explain the opportunity. The mini-value proposition was enough for him or her, but now he or she needs something more substantial than a two-pager but less beefy than the final presentation. Any recommendations? Yes! The *value proposition*. This document tends to run between five and seven pages.

The framework for this document is the same as the other phase 1 tools. But while the first value proposition contained summary information, this extended value proposition includes much of the supporting information behind the rolled-up summary view. This allows others within the target partner organization to conduct their own internal analysis of the information presented and to come to the final meeting loaded with questions and opinions.

One place where extended detail serves you well is in the business justification section. Let's say you have created spreadsheets, made assumptions based on publicly available information, and have arrived at a completely inaccurate view of the monetary payback to the partner. This is still considered to be OK because in the process, the PPO will have the opportunity to see (a) the logic that you employed, (b) the information that was derived from available data, (c) the quality of your research, and (d) the seriousness of the business case from your point of view. Even if the numbers are wrong, the potential partner will usually point out what was inaccurate, giving you incredibly valuable insight as to how products are sold, priced, and maintained through the PPO's service and support contracts. Furthermore, this information does not go to waste. It is employed during the second round of number crunching for a very accurate accounting of the business opportunity, which can be shown to internal management and the partner.

In the case of the firm pitching to American Express, its extended value proposition lengthened the business opportunity section from two short paragraphs to four long paragraphs. Each paragraph was full of significant financial information, which was supported by research, customer feedback, and experience.

The product section is also expanded. The competitive section should include at least one matrix highlighting your product in relation to the competitors' and how this benefits the potential partner. Finally, any visual representation that will show how your product will partner with the PPO's product(s) or company to win over the market is ideal. Using a compare-and-contrast chart of the PPO's status before a partnership and after the partnership, the reader can sometimes grasp in seconds complex working relationships.

In its pitch to American Express, this same company broadened the product discussion from one section to four. Within the product architecture component, it included an illustration that diagramed the product before and after the proposed partnership. The customer benefits were immediately visible as were the dependencies on American Express.

Tips for the Extended Value Proposition

If you have a product that is hard to understand (like laser equipment or communications software), incorporate short sample customer dialogue scenarios. Each scenario must be one paragraph and state how the customer is using the product and the result. Two or three of these will validate to the business manager that customers care about your product, even if a description of the product flies right over his or her head. The last component of the extended value proposition directed to American Express in the preceding example included an entire section with customer testimony.

Also, show industry trends, along with how your business is anticipating those trends and their impact on the potential partner. This information is particularly helpful if you are trying to convey the point that your firm is an innovator of next-generation products, and it needs codevelopment funds. By demonstrating your ability to identify trends and to create products that meet the changing face of consumers' demands and linking your company's expertise in this area to the revenue potential for the partner, you are planting the seeds for a longer-term relationship. In the above example, the outside company gave American Express third-party data from industry market research and forecasting firms as well as benchmarks from customer focus groups.

Refrain from including marketing or sales plans. This is not the time or the audience for this low-level (that is, tactical) information. It is premature and of no interest to the business and product groups that must make a decision on the core components (financial and product) first. If you already have it as an offshoot of the partnership planning exercises, hold onto it. You will be using it, but not now.

Premeeting Brief

Don't rely on your counterpart at the PPO to adequately prepare the attendees. Instead, prepare a *premeeting brief*, which is a document distributed to all individuals attending the first meeting. This document is short (between five and seven pages), and much of the information it contains can be pulled from the interim presentation. The one-sided, double-spaced document includes the logos of each firm in the upper left and right corners. The footer identifies the document as the premeeting brief for the partnership development meeting. Instead of being a bullet-point document, it is composed as running text and provides context and details.

Having a premeeting brief on hand is particularly helpful when you have individuals who decide to attend the meeting at the last minute and have no context in which to understand the partnership proposal. Prevent getting blindsided by an uninformed individual by having extra copies of the brief at the meeting (preferably placed in the middle of the table). If people come in who are obviously clueless, offer them the premeeting brief and say that it will bring them up to speed on the opportunities and reasons behind the meeting. It will at least allow the meeting to continue until they have something intelligent to offer.

The brief includes information leveraged from already created documents or presentations. For example, the purpose of the meeting, the objectives and background of the partnership proposal, and the business opportunity the partnershup will create are all extracted from previous e-mails. The attendees' section identifies the name, title, and role of the individuals at each company who are working on the partnership. This is fabulous information to share on both sides. The agenda should be a separate page that summarizes the information and can be handed out separately.

Two additional sections must be included for the internally distributed premeeting brief. The first is *an organization chart* that connects the decision makers and influencers from the PPO. This will save you from inane questions about who is influencing whom. If you have been keeping an organization chart for the PPO in which you are making notes on the key personnel, be sure to transfer that information to the prebriefing document you are giving to your own in-house personnel.

This is particularly helpful for individuals who have not had the opportunity to participate in the interim presentation or conference call. It is also useful for those who enter the meeting once it has already started, and need to know the roles of the individuals in the room. If you create a more detailed version meant for the eyes of your company only, be sure to delete sensitive information before distributing the generic version at the formal meeting.

The following examples are taken from a five-person manufacturing company's meeting notes prepared as part of a partnership proposal directed to the Sony Corporation. The names have been changed at the request of the manufacturing company and Sony.

> *Bob Jones, VP of operations, definition of the client strategy and discussion of the Sony partnership on a strategic level.*

> *James Markum, director of marketing, communication and explanation of product features, architectural advantages, and point person for technical questions.*

> *Greg Laughin, president and CEO, expression of executive commitment to the Sony strategic and technological initiatives and discussion points of company direction and vision.*

The individuals participating from the Sony group supplied their own role definitions at the request of the alliance manager:

> *Toby Kline, industry marketing manager, strategic contact for [firm] at present and decision maker for business relationships, funding, and support of partners within his industry. Responsible for all applications, tools,*

and enabling technologies at Sony. Areas include Internet, intranet, systems management, decision support, electronic commerce, application management, and all associated enabling technologies.

Denise Peterson, industry marketing, business development, day-to-day contact for [firm] regarding sales, marketing, and professional services activities. Responsible for aggressively promoting partners who move Sony products through the channel.

The second page is a frequently asked questions (FAQ) sheet. If this is the first meeting with a particular organization, individuals will raise a number of questions that stem from their desire to be as prepared as possible.

The number 1 question of all time? In my six years of day-in-and-day-out business development, I have found the number 1 question prior to a meeting is: What do I wear? Do your best to make everyone feel comfortable by determining the dress code. Identify whether the environment is business casual (no ties allowed), which is the norm for technology companies in Silicon Valley, or hot locations like Texas, or formal business for industries in health care or finance (ties required).

It is also beneficial to cover the general tenor of the meeting. For instance, does the PPO manage meetings with a formal style wherein questions are reserved until the end (American Express), or are meetings conducted informally wherein rambunctious personnel are encouraged to interrupt or risk losing their good question, as encouraged by Steve Ballmer, CEO of Microsoft.

Tips on the Premeeting Brief

Depending on the content of the brief, a follow-up coaching session is well worth the additional hour or two. This is particularly the case if few people in the group have either attended partnership development meetings in the past or if the PPO has areas of concern that need to be addressed early. The coaching session will be the perfect opportunity to go through a dry run of the presentation with the right speakers rehearsing their part. Covering sticky issues (or the risks that were identified during the planning stage) is also a smart strategy. Preparing the entire group will not just reduce the potential for conflicts on the part of your team members but it will also empower your group to handle any unanticipated situation with grace and professionalism.

Business Presentation

Producing the final business presentation should be a snap given all the preparatory work you have done from creating the partnership plan to the more condensed version of the value proposition document. The goal of the business presentation meeting is to gain agreement on moving forward to the product due-diligence review stage under the auspices of the partnership you are proposing. Since the business presentation is no more than the interim presentation complete with the changes that have been requested by the PPO's business manager, it should be a snap to prepare. The only added components will be the written-out descriptions of the key points associated with each slide.

The best presentations are those conveying confidence and conviction. This means delivering something more than a reading of the words on the page. And believe me, many trained CEOs, vice presidents, and alliance managers suffer from stage fright and revert to reading the presentation. If you see this tendency in any of the presenters (including yourself), a coaching session prior to the meeting is a *must*.

Tips on the Business Presentation

While you are giving the presentation, deliver no more than two messages per slide even if the text on the page may have five bullet points or a graphical illustration. Remember that statistics show that audience members retain no more than two or three messages at most. Stating only the two most important points for each slide will give the audience an interactive dynamic of listening to you and then looking to the written-out version for the supporting text.

Second, do *not* hand out the presentation before the meeting. Everyone will start reading the materials and not pay attention to the speaker. It is much better to provide handouts (such as technical product materials) that can address a particular product question that might be raised. Instead, pass out the presentation at the end of the meeting if you must. Be sure this booklet is double-sided and shows two slides per page, with the slides reproduced in black and white versions. Otherwise, keep as much information to yourself as you can. Your business manager counterpart can have a copy (after you have made it a PDF read-only file) as a follow-up. A ploy that never works well is to ask for everyone's e-mail address so that you can send the presentation to them directly. This is unprofessional and will only serve to irritate the meeting participants.

Pass the shoe. Not the buck, the shoe. Imagine yourself playing a game of craps and you want someone else to have a turn. Partnership development has a few gambling elements to it, and others will want a chance to roll the dice. If you are doing too much talking, ask other team members to address questions: "I'll let John answer that." This is a seamless way to get others involved in the conversation. It's not unreasonable to think that some questions will simply be inappropriate to answer.

The best line I've ever heard was from Jeff Miller, the chairman and former CEO of information management provider of Documentum Software. I attended a meeting during which he was getting grilled by a member of the press about a particular customer. He responded by saying that "the information was unavailable" to him at that moment but that he would ask his vice president of sales if the question was still of interest at the end of the call. The reporter felt acknowledged because an offer was made to follow up on the question that was promptly forgotten.

Phase 2   Partnership Development Tools:
The Product Presentation

The goal of this meeting is to provide enough information so the product decision makers may validate the opportunity on the table and be inspired to visualize a few new ones. This is known as "getting to Wow." It must be the stated goal of your own internal team.

The presentation should include each aspect that will capture the PPO's attention and inspire discussion, debate, and a worthwhile whiteboarding session.

Presentation Format

The format of this presentation is slightly different from the business presentation. It includes the summary of the partnership proposal but then delves into the product presentation, architectural aspects relevant to the partnership, product integration and/or licensing or design issues, and the proposed product due-diligence review. Within this agenda, the potential partner is asked to participate in the discussion by contributing its own plans. Without the PPO's input, the conversation will be limited as will the value of the meeting.

This presentation is typically much longer than the business presentation. It can easily run from 45 to 65 slides, not including hidden or background slides. The speaker should deliver the information as if he or she were serving a dinner. The presentation should start with a small, easy-to-digest course, followed by subsequent entrées, leaving the dessert for last. By the time it is finished, the recipients are feeling intellectually full and are willing to pay the bill!

Presentation Framework

1. Partnership proposal summary
   a. One page on the discussions to date
   b. One page on the revenue and/or business opportunity (WIIFM again)
   c. One page covering feedback from the PPO and what needs to be covered during the product meeting to continue
   d. Agenda for the rest of the meeting (This will set the time frames, expectations, and meeting overview in case the room has so many attendees that you run out of hard copies of the agenda—which can and does happen if the value proposition did its job!)
2. Product presentation and demonstration
   a. One page on the product or solution—what it does, how it is positioned, and its place in the market
   b. One page on how the product works today (and services the customer) and how it could look tomorrow (through a partnership). (This snapshot should grab their attention and set the stage for the next slide.)
   c. One page on the details of the product—what it uses, how it is designed, how its primary attributes serve the customer
   d. Customer examples (The best way to do this is to list four or five bullet points of monetary payback that a customer will achieve by using your firm's product. If you don't have this information, keep a one-bullet item for each customer, but include other results, expected or real.)
   e. Competitive matrix and advantages
   f. How it integrates with and uses the partner's product line

3. Architectural designs

   This is where lots and lots of slides can exist. A slide for each facet might be appropriate with hidden slides to allow the conversation to go as deeply into the guts of the product as necessary.

4. Presentation and demonstration of (company's) product

   a. One page addressing the state of the product (on the market, pricing, and so on)

   b. One page setting up the demonstration (what they are about to see)—how it will work, where they need to pay attention, and the like

5. Product integration discussion

   a. A page that transitions into working with the partner—to get from here to there, we need to do this and that

   b. A section on the considerations to the partner's product, opportunities identified, issues and recommendations. (Again, this section can have a number of pages, but it's important to fill the group with ideas, so that when they deliver their presentation to the PPO, some of the opportunities can be addressed.)

One mistake companies make during both the business and product presentations is to confuse both with an analyst presentation. This is particularly common among CEOs and vice presidents who are used to going out on the media circuit and regurgitating everything there is to know about a market—the trends, the needs, and so on. Product managers and engineers need to know about their customer and why your product is important. They do not need your view of the history of the market. Be sure to pull this type of information out of the presentation if it happens to find its way in.

Tips for the Product Presentation

Keep the primary presentation core to the central message of gaining agreement on the product direction. There is a fine line between having lots of good information and too much information that will be lost on the audience.

To ensure that the audience is engaged, periodically check the audience for pointers. About every section or so, ask one of the decision makers if the information is at the right level, the speed of the presentation is good for the group, if more detail is desired, and so on. You can essentially make your way around the room to make sure you are meeting the agenda of each individual in the audience.

Do not let yourself get taken down a side path. You want to control the dialogue and not skip over information that will be important to the group. Make sure to acknowledge a point, as with the business presentation, but *instead of completely pushing it off, state the short answer* (for example, "Yes it does do that, and I will explain that feature during the demonstration"), and then continue with your presentation. Product or engineering professionals are a lot less likely to stick around for the actual explanation unless they get a short answer right up front and center.

Incorporate the partner's product if at all possible for the product presentation or demonstration. This may take some doing and might not be appropriate or possible for the first product meeting. However, it certainly does make a statement to the PPO in two ways. First, it shows that you have initiative and can get things done without the PPO's help or guidance. Second, it shows that the partnership is more than a theory. It's real and possible today. It's amazing how much incorporating the PPO's product can impact the speed of discussion—tangible is always better than intangible. Some minds just can't stretch too far.

Do not have a single speaker talking the entire time. Mix it up. Most product meetings will have three to five individuals from both sides present. Each person in the room should have a purpose and a role. If a person doesn't have a role, he or she shouldn't be in the room, period. Nothing says desperation or lack of delegation more clearly than having warm but useless bodies in the room.

The business lead (you) should give the first part of the presentation. This is your turf as the person who has led the discussions to this point. You next acknowledge the role and importance of the product teams and then pass the baton to the senior product manager from your group, who will talk about the product and give the first part of the demonstration. A senior engineer or technical person can give both the last part of the demonstration and lead the discussion on the guts of the product. Depending on others in the room, it can shift back to you for the product integration aspect, or the CTO (chief technology officer, or most senior engineer—a fourth person) can go through the partner integration work, the future, and the needs.

With a two- to three-hour agenda where both sides will be presenting, breaks are going to be needed. You *must* get through the product demonstration before you allow a break of even two minutes. If you don't make it this far, it's hard to get people to stay since they can flit away and not come back.

If you pull together your presentation and have too much content before the product demonstration, trim it down into hidden slides, or move some content to follow the product demonstration. You can easily do this by saying you are not going to tell them about the product first, but rather show them the product and talk through the details afterwards.

A rule of thumb is the 40-minute rule. No one wants to sit for this amount of time without seeing a product, particularly in a product meeting. During the dry-run sessions (during which you must have just as much material as you plan to give during the actual business presentation), time this segment to be sure the speaker(s) can make it within the 40-minute time frame.

Interim Proposal

At the conclusion of the first product meeting, you should have a nice list of comments both positive and (constructively) negative about what you presented. Typically, the partnership is not going to be a slam dunk, sorry to say. Something invariably needs to be done on one or both sides to create the relationship. If this involves product changes, the consequence is a dollar requirement as well as some type of support from the other side to make the product changes according to the specifications of the PPO. This is the purpose behind the next two interim milestones—which are the product proposals.

The *product proposal* is the presentation that incorporates much of the work from the due-diligence review. This presentation is the synthesis of the many exercises required during the phase 2 macro-process. It includes multiple product scenarios—the impact to both organizations from a product perspective first and then from a business (sales and marketing) perspective. The presentation identifies the requirements in terms of personnel and dollars. Ultimately, this information is wrapped up into a proposal and delivered to the business manager from the PPO, who will provide important feedback to you before the final presentation.

During or shortly following the interim presentation to the business manager, who should now be your strong advocate within the PPO, you should make sure that all the points raised during the product meeting were addressed. Feedback on the feasibility of the scenarios presented, dependencies, and issues or conflicts within the PPO pertaining to those scenarios are also identified.

Presentation Framework

This proposal is similar to the initial product presentation but not quite as long. The intent is to provide an overview of the recommended solutions to the issues raised and the implications to both firms. This is the key information. The "how's" will be raised when the rest of the team members from the PPO can respond and ask questions during the formal product proposal meeting.

Presentation Framework to Be Reviewed during the Interim Conference Call

1. Recap of discussions to date (action items from the last meeting)
2. Recommended solutions (and scenarios)
   a. Logic behind the scenarios
   b. Implications to the potential partner
3. Path for progression (requirements from the potential partner)
4. Timelines and costs

Tips on the Interim Presentation

Because this is an abbreviated version of the final proposal, it is natural to expect questions regarding "the how." These questions arise from the desire to understand if major requirements will be placed on the PPO's organization. Answer to the degree that will make the PPO comfortable and give it a sense of confidence about the direction you are proposing. But don't get into the nitty-gritty of the meeting. Don't give away too much detail. This might lead the technical manager to determine that the entire team doesn't need to reassemble, and this isn't the outcome you desire.

Final Proposal

Preparing the final product proposal requires building onto the framework started for the interim presentation. The final proposal has more supporting detail, and it is designed to not generate ideas but rather to arrive at a definitive conclusion so that the partnership agreement can get started. For this reason the scenarios painted must naturally lead the audience to prefer one over another.

Final Proposal Framework

1. Recap of discussions to date
   a. Action items from the last meeting
   b. Original business opportunities identified
   c. Associated business outcomes (market share, money, and so on)
2. Recommended solutions snapshot
   a. Choices that were reviewed and final recommendations
   b. Payback to both firms based on the final recommendations
   c. Requirements for each organization (product only at this point)
3. Logic behind the scenarios (Parse out each issue that was raised—the options, challenges, and outcomes. This section needs to be bullet-point, straightforward product discussion.)
4. Implications to the partner
   a. Benefits to the recommended solution
      i. Competitive advantages
      ii. Customer benefits
      iii. Partner network benefits
   b. Challenges with the solution and means to overcome them—possible product changes required and details supporting this work
   c. Short- and long-term product opportunities that will be generated from the initial scenario
      i. Sales opportunities that can be identified, and examples supporting this expectation
      ii. Market leadership that can be projected, and spreadsheets supporting this projection
5. Path for progression, with a partnership roll-out plan (executive summary first)
   a. Project plans supporting partnership plan
   b. Marketing and sales plan supporting partnership plan
6. Requirements from the potential partner, summary view
   a. Personnel (product, program, engineers, and so on)
   b. Marketing dollars, programs
   c. Sales training, and so on

7. Timelines and costs, shown with a graphic that projects the course of the plan (Three to six months is normal, and anything beyond six months is intimidating at the beginning of a relationship.)

Tips for the Final Proposal

A lot of information has been compiled over a multiweek period of time by your team, which is versed inside and out on the logic behind the proposal. You are giving this information to a group that has probably thought about your company twice, for 10 seconds each time, since the last meeting. Expect lots of questions, and ask lots of questions.

You need to bring the group along step by step through the discovery process in a relatively short period of time. And then you are expecting the participants to feel comfortable enough to give some solid feedback. This is a lot to ask even from the best and brightest.

During phase 2, provide a two-week lead time for the financial and technical teams prior to their involvement. This time will enable each individual to clear schedules and meet a deliverable date. Also, ask your partner contact for sample documents, such as contracts and planning or reporting sheets that might be used. This gives the legal department the opportunity to review the partnership plans well ahead of the time when the documents are actually needed.

Last, don't be afraid to share the project plan and timeline with the partner (at the high level). This is a team effort, and trust must be built and maintained throughout this potentially long and intense process. This can be accomplished only by collaborating with your partner.

To ensure that nothing is missed for the partnership program management plan, make sure you have answered the following questions:

- Does the final proposal convey the overall objectives of the partnership development efforts?
- Are the activities, owners, and due dates clearly identified?
- Are dependencies reflected in the plan?
- Have the contributors provided estimated due dates and validation of ownership?
- Has the right management from all participating divisions been made aware of contributions expected from their group? And are they educated about the intent and support of the efforts?

- Does the plan reflect financial milestones and results?
- Have you identified the date and method for updated plans to be distributed in advance of the weekly project update meeting?
- Does the plan take into consideration outside organizations that affect the outcome?
- Have you determined how comments, changes, and approvals will be captured (either in notes in the project plan or inserted comments in *Excel*?)
- Are the plan recipients proficient in using the project plan software application?
- Have you included monthly executive updates starting with phase 2?

Phase 3 Tools

During the last phase of the partnership development process, the only tools to be used are agreement templates. Depending on the type of partnership created, a specific agreement will be used that includes the terms and conditions required by each organization. The previous chapter on structuring partnership agreements detailed the various informal and formal partnership agreements used during the third phase of the partnership development process.

Once you have chosen the type of agreement, negotiated the terms to your satisfaction, and signed the document, the relationship is ready to be transitioned from the active partnership development or creation process to the partnership management efforts. The next and final chapter covers the three aspects critical to producing significant shareholder returns through partnerships.

10

Partnering Techniques for the Long-Term Relationship

CHAPTER HIGHLIGHTS

- *Overcoming conflicts*
- *Techniques for succeeding with your partner*
- *Managing barriers within your own organization*
- *What not to do and say to the potential partner*

FRANCISCO FRANCO, the Basque general responsible for creating and breaking numerous political alliances during the early twentieth century, can be seen as the prototypical alliance manager. Franco wore the mask of partnership for his alliance *du jour*, which, according to the *Basque History of the World* by Mark Hurlansky, included wearing the clothes best reflecting his alliances: the red beret of Carlism when in northern Spain and the black shirt of fascism when in southern Spain. Each outfit signaled an attempt to avoid a potential conflict with regional leaders opposed to his wartime agenda.

It is unlikely that wearing the logo-embroidered oxford shirt of your most favored partner will eliminate much conflict. Yet, you will have to be creative when you are faced with the task of managing the newly formed partnership. There will be a host of new issues to resolve with the partner, your coworkers, management, and the board. And let's not forget the customers, partners, and vendors who are impacted by your relationship with the partner. As the go-to person for the alliance(s), you are responsible and accountable for the perception and interaction these communities have with either party in the partnership.

This final chapter discusses the best practices for building long-term partnership relationships. The most successful alliance managers focus on getting a job with a company that embodies a pro-partnering attitude. The best alliance managers know how to resolve conflicts but also how to prevent conflicts from arising in the first place. In between are many direct pieces of advice from those who are soliciting partnerships and those who have been solicited. CEOs of both micro-enterprises and billion-dollar enterprises have taken the time to provide some of their best tips for creating the best partnership possible, and some of those tips are given here.

Getting the Job by Interviewing the Management Team

Nothing can be worse than becoming the manager, director, or executive responsible for alliances at a firm not endowed with a pro-partnering attitude, but that is exactly what Frank Artale, former vice president at VERITAS Software encountered when he started. Yet his experience of working in hostile environments while at Microsoft served him well when he worked with Kris Hagerman and CEO Gary Blume to change the culture at VERITAS Software. Hired within 12 months of one another, they united to become an effective force of behavioral guidance in what was a neutral partnering environment at best and antagonistic at worst. According to Artale, the hardest part was changing the culture of seeking short-term revenue to seeking longer-term results. "We had to fundamentally shift the thinking from the deal of the day to understanding the key relationships that were going to drive the company forward one and two years down the road."

One way you can identify the attitude of the PPO's management is to look at its marketing literature. Actify's CEO Mike Walsh believes that any company "presenting itself as a one-stop shopping solution is going to be more difficult to get through." One example of this is

Apple Computers. Apple itself provides the software, operating system, hardware, and the chip for its computer products. Internally, it acts as its own conglomerate of partnerships. Apple had the opportunity to be Microsoft, but instead it chose to sell a completely integrated solution, and in doing so, it has missed out on the flexibility afforded by a company not confined to a closed environment. So while profitable, it is not the dominant market leader it could have been.

If you are not a part of the executive team, query your management about their general attitude toward alliances. Don't take for granted a pro-partnering environment simply because an alliance manager's job is open. In choosing a company to work for, one quality to look for is the ability to effect change throughout the organization. Specifically, will you be able to push a new partnership agenda into the field and encourage change within departmental structures to better align with alliance goals.

The "A" Player and True Belief

As you evaluate the management team of a PPO, remember they are also evaluating you. Based on client and partner feedback over the years, I have found that passion is the number 1 trait of a successful alliance manager. Passion leads to motivation, which results in overcoming obstacles, which leads to achieving objectives. It's that simple. Persistence, the byproduct of passion, pays off more than the ability to be articulate or even to show an understanding of the objectives.

It is this persistence that will lead you to uncover the metrics of the potential partner. It is the belief in the partnership that will encourage you to plan for, justify, ask for, and receive an increased program budget when the other group budgets are getting slashed. You know that of all the groups in the company, it is yours alone that is endowed with the ability to impact every other organization. Nothing more than your confidence in this belief will see you through the internal barriers that are placed in your way.

Once You're Hired: Managing Conflict

Every alliance manager will tell you that the most disruptive conflicts are those starting with mundane errors that escalate unchecked until they reach the executive corner office. Tactical errors can feed into hurricane-force destructive powers. One such error occurred when a "press release was sent prematurely without quote approval," cites Microsoft SQL Server business manager Steve Murchie. In this case, the error led to a public retraction by the partner as well as by a leading industry analyst firm who had written a lengthy report based on the press release. It was embarrassing for everyone involved and highly damaging for the alliance manager.

The second most common cause of conflict is product certification announcements that are inaccurate. While this seems almost unbelievable to product development folks, it happens all the time, largely due to an overzealous marketing team. Regardless, conflict erupts between multiple groups at both companies as legal departments quickly become involved to undo the damage.

Missed deadlines are the third most visible source of partner conflict. While not as serious as the other two conflict sources, it is the most common, and in the long term, it is more destructive to a relationship.

Resolving Conflict without Blame

The most effective means of handling conflict with the partner is to address the issue in as direct a manner as possible. Separating the personal relationship between yourself and your alliance manager counterpart is equally important in healing the wounds of conflict.

Phillip Benz of Advanced Vascular Dynamics has had his share of conflicts and has found that the conflicts handled directly are easier to dismiss. He has provided an example of working with a publicly traded partner who attributed a product delay to Advanced Vascular. Benz learned about the partner's claim from the newswire first, his CEO second, and the rest of his internal team third. The partner's actions caused a communications headache that wasn't alleviated by the knowledge that his product had been shipped off months before and had nothing to do with the partner's own internal sins.

Had this partner come forward and acknowledged to Benz that something was amiss, Benz might have prepared a statement for the press. As it was, Benz's peer blithely reasoned that Benz's company wouldn't be impacted by negative press the same way as would a public firm.

In this situation, the conflict was not managed directly, and the consequences were minor. In another example between two very large software companies, the results were nearly disastrous. Several years ago, five of the world's largest software firms were working together on a promotional CD to send to a select group of several thousand customers. This venture was the first of its kind for everyone involved, and the alliance managers were working around the clock to get the right software on the CD within the given time frame. As one software firm was responsible for managing the coordination and the packaging of the software, its testing group discovered a joke line of code within one of the submissions. It read "Microsoft is the evil empire, death to all non-borgs." This might have been rather funny except for the fact that the firm pulling the effort together was, in fact, Microsoft.

The debacle might have all blown over quickly had the alliance manager from the offending company reacted appropriately about the entire issue. Instead of falling on the extended sword, the manager issued forth a wave of denials, attributions, and conjectures. The manager's reaction served only to infuriate the Microsoft program manager and cause the delay of the CD. Had the alliance manager employed classic conflict resolution techniques by being direct without making it personal, the incident would have been overshadowed by a broader focus on the intent of the partnership.

The Direct Approach to Resolving Conflict

Laurie Erickson relates a great story about a conflict she had with one of her long-term manufacturers in France. She and her colleagues had just created a new design process by laminating denim directly onto hair clips. She had flown to France to share this new process with the manufacturer, and she left a few sample pieces behind. No sooner had she returned to America than she received a call from the manufacturer. It turned out Erickson's primary competitor was in France the day after Erickson's visit, and her manufacturer sold the samples and the process to her competitor. The manufacturer claimed that once produced, it had the rights to the manufacturing process even though it was Erickson's firm that had provided the intellectual property.

Because of Erickson's trust-based relationships with the manufacturers, it never occurred to her that the firm would be in a position to give her designs to a competitor. But the partner defended its position. "You are still making money if I sell it to her just as if I were selling it to a retail store," he argued. Erickson had to go through the exhaustive process of describing that market leadership is sometimes about *industry perception*, brand awareness, and positioning. Unfortunately, the soft conflict resolution approach didn't appear to work.

"I had them go back and compare my growth against my competitor's. Then I asked who they thought was really going to come up with the more innovative products to spur sales." To drive the point home, Erickson then rhetorically asked where they wanted to be as a business in 15 years. Within 24 hours, the manufacturer had repealed its offer to the competitor, which was highly embarrassing but preserved the relationship with Erickson. "They are used to selling a collection for a short term," Erickson summarized. "I sell for a long term."

Reacting in the Heat of the Moment

Erickson wisely started her conflict resolution with logic and reason. This line of reasoning evolved to a subtle threat to change manufacturing partners, which luckily was not necessary in the end. A good many more conflicts would be resolved if alliance managers could keep their cool in the heat of the moment. Unfortunately, a propensity to take a misguided statement personally flavored with stress overcomes good sense.

Don't let this happen to you. Protect the investment put forth by managing even the most heated situations through the use of deflection, diplomacy, and constructive application of a comment. Even the most derogatory comment can be nullified if managed properly.

One way to nullify a negative comment is to turn it into an offer. Dale Bathum of Bite Footwear was told by a partner that his product was "uncool." Even so, the partner wanted to work with Bathum's company. Without blinking an eye, Bathum responded by asking for the partner's help in "making their product cool." The partner felt its comment was acknowledged and eagerly agreed to assist in any way possible. Ironically, when the products came to market, consumer response vindicated Bite Footwear as the "brand to beat" while the partner's product was perceived as "behind the times."

Inventors or product developers of any type tend to become more personally sensitive to derogatory comments, particularly those aimed at their products. While hard, these comments cannot be taken personally. Criticism can be many things depending on who's in the room. For example, a criticism of your product might be the means through which the PPO alliance manager gains a favor with its own engineering team. On the other hand, it might be a way for the alliance manager to set up his or her firm for a better negotiating position. If the criticism is raised by a product manager from the PPO, it might simply be a test of your confidence in your own product line.

Handle these arrows with the graceful side step. Never raise your voice, shake your head in a dismissive manner, or smirk. All of these nonverbal cues are more insulting that a direct negative response. You absolutely must maintain eye contact with the person talking, lean forward as if you really care, and even go as far as to take notes. These simple tactics show you have the dignity to be polite even if the person on the other side of the table is a raving lunatic.

Instead of reacting, dig deeper into the wound. This will uncover if the rant can be substantiated or if it's a smokescreen. You can politely ask if these issues have been discussed internally. If a claim about your product has been made that you know to be false, don't bother to refute it. Instead, ask for the "third-party source" of the information. If the statement was fabricated or the benchmarks were conducted internally, the speaker will be forced to admit this in a public setting. You can then state a desire to see the results so that you can address the problem immediately.

At the executive level, this kind of interaction is highly unusual. In working with the chief executives of large and small companies alike over the years, I have rarely heard snide offhand remarks made. In fact, the atmosphere is more collegial than anything else. It is at the product and alliance manager levels where the conflict takes place. Yet it is also where resolutions are created and the partnership bond formed and strengthened.

Being the Diplomat

Effectively managing difficult situations doesn't imply weakness. You just have to know when to walk away from a deal instead of walking further into it. This philosophy applies equally to agreement negotiation and conflict resolution. In a trust-based relationship, both sides are motivated to succeed. This means that there is going to be compromise. You must indicate the point at which the partnership is no longer worth your time and energy.

Diplomacy means training yourself and your team how to convey thoughts and opinions in a more reasonable and less offensive manner than your partner. This behavioral guidance will at least keep you out of potential defamation lawsuits. For example, instead of saying, "That's the most hare-brained idea in the planet," try, "That's a bit off our chosen course, but it's something we can consider." Rather than saying, "We thought about that, and it simply won't work," Try, "Let's explore a few of the possible implications so that I can clearly understand your thinking." Instead of saying, "I developed that product, and what you are saying is incorrect," say. "Let me see if I've interpreted your issue correctly."

Stepping over the Alliance Manager

When you have tried your best conflict resolution maneuvers and played the role of diplomat and things still haven't gotten better, you need to apply to executive sponsorship. This is a silver bullet because it's usually good for only one time. Unfortunately, too many use it as the first course of conflict resolution, and they therefore get poor results.

Silver bullets do one thing very well. They get the first meeting. No product manager is going to refuse a request from an executive vice president to "listen to their story." Thus, silver bullets can be the impetus to resurrect a badly damaged relationship.

Preventive Medicine

The best conflict management strategy is to ensure that very little arises in the first place. This is very easily done. Set expectations appropriately, deliver on commitments, and don't use strong-arm tactics that get you the agreement you desire but at a price so high that the motivation to work with your firm undermines the written contract. In other words, annoy them, but don't make them mad.

A first start is to underpromise and overdeliver. Companies that bluff, exaggerate, or overrepresent what their product can do are setting themselves up for failure. This sounds like common sense, but according to Murchie, the majority of verbal pitches he has received are "so unbelievable I just didn't want to spend the time." He provided an example in which one person was pushing a partnership in the nonprofit arena. This individual was trying to show how Microsoft could make an additional $500 million through a partnership with his firm. It's hard to recall a single entity in the world making that kind of money in a space defined as not-for-profit.

Instead, do your homework on the partner's product. Understand the technology, mechanics, ingredients, fabrics, processes, and issues faced by the partner. Don't send a query for a partnership to the PPO if a similar partnership exists with your competitor in the same target market.

Prevent conflicts in the courtroom by identifying up front if you are currently competitive to your potential partner. This doesn't mean you won't get an audience. Both Advanced Vascular Dynamics and Pro Clarity received and got an audience as well as a subsequent partnership with their main competitors. What you want to avoid at all costs is pretending to be complementary when you know full well the products overlap.

Internal Conflict

The partnership community an alliance manager supports stretches far and wide. This is equally true within his or her own organization. Barriers are erected from every group required to support your efforts— engineering can't spare the resources, marketing doesn't have the budget, product development is booked out 18 months, and operations isn't interested in outsourcing. In the face of these arguments, you must marry your passion and belief in the partnership with logical arguments that support your position.

Budget Allocations

Even in the best economy, discretionary budgets are thin. Remind your finance department that partnership development is not discretionary or optional. It is paramount to the success of your company. Based on the work you completed during the partnership planning exercise, submit a reasonable budget based on your projections. Point out that the partnership requires the resources necessary to accomplish the tactical requirements but also to realize long-term goals. In so doing, you effectively put the finance manager in a corner. After all, the reason for creating the partnership in the first place is to generate revenue opportunities, control costs, extend market penetration, and deliver shareholder value.

Guiding Lights of Partner Development

You may be armed with the best plan, supported by intelligent and capable people, and your programs financed through the end of the year. But keep in mind your partnership development guiding lights. Those are the beams of clarity you can call upon to keep your focus clear and direction unwavering even in the most challenging of times.

I've selected a few gems I have heard over the years as a starting point for your own list:

Actively look for people who can make your life easier—Dale Bathum, CEO, Bite Footware

A partnership is about making the customers happy. At the end of the day, what's really important to the customer is that both products work together, and do so seamlessly. Hiding the dissonance that naturally occurs in a partnership is critical.—Kris Hagerman, EVP Strategic Operations, VERITAS Software

Customers are partners in our business since some of our customers have been around for decades. We didn't know 30 years ago that one rookie cop would now be a police captain, but we do know he values his relationship with us.—Mark Blumenthal, CEO, Blumenthal

Culture and values have to align well and core competencies have to align perfectly or a partnership won't succeed.—Mark Anderson, CEO, Anderson Hay and Grain

They Can Do It, So Can You

Creating a product, launching a business, and starting a new vocation takes guts. It also takes a passion and belief in the impact your efforts will have on your company, your consumer, or better yet, society as a whole. It's exciting to think partnerships can truly impact the average person. A single manufacturing partnership brings a new medical equipment device to market at a reduced cost. A joint development partnership produces a new health food cracker that lowers cholesterol and blood pressure. A licensing partnership reduces road rage by uniting map directions through in-car and Internet-based navigation systems. A distribution agreement makes our cars safer by enabling engineers from all over the world to share information via large-scale drawings.

Most of these partnerships were created with complementary partners while a few were the product of alliances with competitors. It says a lot when a small firm can stare the highest-risk partner scenario in the eye and win like Phillip Benz of Advanced Vascular Dynamics: "We make 90 percent of the products in a market space, and we did it through a partnership with our largest competitor."

A single partnership had the power to increase margins and profits as it pushed the cost of goods down. It accelerated the time to creating and delivering new innovation to the consumer while leveraging the resources of one team with those of another. Ultimately, value was created and realized across every organization within the company. This translated into dramatically increased shareholder return. And that's the promise of partnerships. It is happening today for many companies, and it can happen for you.

GLOSSARY

ACCELERATORS: Contractual incentives tied into a dollar figure. Accelerators are incentives used to shorten the length of time it takes to create a partnership. They are also used as additional compensation if performance metrics are exceeded.

ALLIANCE MANAGER: The individual responsible for creating and managing a partnership.

ALLIANCEMAPPING: A model designed to identify a company's ability to create successful partnerships, based on determining the company's product capabilities, available financing, and partnership goals.

ASSETS: In partnership development, usually the intellectual property, patent, and trademark assets of the PPOs. Only during phase 3 of the partnership development life cycle does the term *assets* refer to physical (personnel and property) and financial (bank account) holdings.

BANDWIDTH: The amount of personnel resources available from either potential partner organization for a particular project. A person's individual "bandwidth" refers to how much time he or she can devote to a project.

BENCHMARK: Testing procedure used to validate the operating functions of a product. There are both *internal benchmarks*, or those required by the PPOs, and *external benchmarks*, or those required by third parties.

BIDIRECTIONAL: Benefitting both parties. A nondisclosure agreement is bidirectional as it protects the confidentiality of both parties.

BUNDLING: Putting two products together to sell to the market.

BUNDLING, SOFT: Packaging two independent products to be sold together but wrapped separately—for example, a radio sold with batteries "included." The batteries are wrapped separately and shown to the consumer with a packaging element distinct from the radio.

BUNDLING, HARD: Packaging two independent products to be sold together and wrapped together with or without acknowledgment—for example, a car is sold with an independently manufactured radio already installed.

BUSINESS CASE OR PROPOSITION: The basic business justification for creating a partnership relationship. The business case can be made as a financial or competitive strategy.

CIRCLE OF INFLUENCE: The outside forces that assist in decision making. Depending on the phase of the partnership development strategy and planning, the circle of influence can resemble any of the following examples: the individuals that are necessary to make a decision, the type of companies that have horizontal or vertical relationships with an organization, or the type of products that are purchased by a particular type of consumer.

CLOSED-LOOP CYCLE: A cycle in which a process is followed, and the outcome results are then reincorporated into the process. This continual refinement improves efficiency, shortens the partnership development cycle, and delivers a predictable outcome when the cycle has been completed enough times to deliver trends.

COMARKETING AGREEMENT: An agreement that outlines exactly what each company will do to market a product or service for the partnership.

COMMERCIAL AGREEMENT: A type of agreement by which the partnership is structured such that one party is paying the other. For example, a distribution agreement is a type of commercial agreement. However, a marketing agreement, by which both firms are working on different aspects of marketing the relationship, or products associated with the relationship, is not considered a commercial agreement.

CORE COMPETENCY: A unique and fundamental specialty of the company, usually referring to a product it produces.

DEFINITIVE AGREEMENT: A final, formal contractual agreement.

CONSIDERATION: The initial amount to be paid to one partner at the start of the partnership agreement.

DUE-DILIGENCE PROCESS: The process of validating product and company information.

DISTRIBUTION AGREEMENT: A document that legally authorizes one party to sell, or distribute, a product or service by another party.

GO-TO-MARKET SOLUTION: A product or service that has all the required components to be a complete solution for the consumer, specifically from the initial product to the setup, use, and servicing. For instance, a paint manufacturer creates paint, has a partner to distribute the paint to retailers, has another firm to offer training to painting companies, and then has a partnership with a home installer to ensure quality control and satisfaction. Two companies together might be able to offer a go-to-market solution for a particular industry.

EMBEDDED AGREEMENT: A type of licensing agreement that gives a company the rights to include another company's product within its own offering. An example of an embedded agreement is a toy company's contract to sell toys with a specific tie-in to a newly released feature film.

ENGAGEMENT SCENARIO: The way that partnering companies work together on a daily basis.

EXECUTIVE BRIEFING SESSION: A forum for a PPO's upper-level management on the partnership development status. A prime opportunity to gain access to the executives of another organization, or for their own executives to create a peer relationship with a partner. Held regionally or at a corporate office, it is also a vehicle to give input to key strategic initiatives and determine how a closer alliance could be formed. These forums are not usually posted or announced publicly.

HISTORICAL PRECEDENCE: The use of a previous partnership as an example to predict the outcome of a partnership in the making.

HOLD-BACK: A contractual obligation by which a portion of the final payment is retained until a particular term is met.

HOLD-BACK, DOUBLE: A second contractual obligation by which a portion of the payment is retained for the duration of the agreement.

INDUSTRY MANAGER: An individual responsible for managing an industry focus within a company, such as the health care industry or the financial industry.

JOINT DEVELOPMENT: Two or more companies working together to enhance an existing product or create a new product for market. The companies, patents, tools, and so on are individually owned and not shared with the other firm.

JOINT VENTURE: An arrangement by which two or more companies are contributing resources into a new company that will create a product or service.

LEVERAGED PARTNER MODEL: (*a*) A partnership development plan in which the overall effort is accelerated. For example, company C works with company A on conducting a due-diligence review, and it passes the information to company B, eliminating the need to go through the review again. (*b*) The term can also be used when a partner uses its own network in such a way that it doesn't need to create new alliances with each firm.

LICENSING AGREEMENT: An agreement by which one company is permitted to use the assets of another company to create a new product or service.

MASTER AGREEMENT: A document used in partnerships to allocate areas in which the partners' products complement, overlap, or compete with one another. This agreement contains the positioning, messaging, pricing, and other terms necessary for the sales and marketing teams of both organizations to communicate consistently with customers, the media, and other external and internal entities.

MICRO-ENTERPRISE: A business with fewer than five employees.

MONETIZE: To define the monetary value of an activity or effort.

NONDISCLOSURE AGREEMENT: A document that binds the parties from divulging the contents of their meetings or discussions for a stated period of time.

NONPERFORMANCE PENALTIES: A term used in agreements to specify the negative consequences for not meeting deliverables associated with a partnership agreement.

NO-TOUCH ACTIVITY: An action that does not require human intervention.

PARTNERSHIP MODEL: A hypothetical business plan for creating a partnership.

Path for progression: A plan or road map that outlines the desired evolution of a partnership.

Payout terms: The payment schedule and amounts stipulated in a partnership agreement.

Performance incentives: Payments associated with overachieving objectives of the partnerships. Most often they take the form of financial incentives, but they can also be allocated as in-kind services, such as marketing events, brochure creations, or cooperative advertising.

Performance measurements: Metrics that are used to assess the success of a partnership.

Potential partner organization (PPO): A firm that is a possible partner.

Predictable outcomes: The results expected from a potential partnership. Usually only used with historical data or historical precedence.

Press release: A document distributed to the media that announces company news.

Right of first refusal: A contractual agreement by which one party is given the opportunity to override a specified deal that the other party may attempt to make over the lifetime of the contract. For example, company A has the right of first refusal in an agreement with its premier partner, company B, to review and approve any partnership company B may be considering.

Royalties: Payments made for the use of someone else's intellectual property according to the terms in a licensing and distribution agreement. Usually, royalties are paid as an advance payment to which is added a certain amount for each unit sold.

Silver bullet: A single-use striking force. In partnership maintenance, this term is applied to the use of an executive contact, usually a CEO or other high-placed individual, whose direction can cause doors to open immediately.

Strategic imperative: A motivating factor that puts pressure on an organization to make a decision. Normally, this is an economic, business, or competitive strategy.

TECHNICAL ALIGNMENT: The way in which products, or processes, of the participants in a partnership work together.

TIERING: Defining and ranking an outside firm as a potential partner based on internal company criteria.

VALUE DRIVEN: Motivated by the desire to create value for a particular company.

VALUE PROPOSITION: Information added to a business proposition to describe why one firm is pursuing a partnership with another firm. This added information usually pertains to financial, competitive, and strategic gains anticipated for the PPO.

Index

Acknowledgments

DAVID KIRKPATRICK of *Fortune* deserves many kudos for being the first to catch the partnership vision, and the same must go to Chris Caggiano of *Inc. Magazine* for bringing the vision to small businesses. I owe gratitude to my agent, Matt Wagner, for his enthusiasm, guidance, and education about the partnering concept, and to Janice Race, "the peach," for incredible patience during the editing cycle. Mary Glenn receives high marks for brutal candor, which improved the quality of the book, while Pam Liflander's soft touch sped the process along. Thanks to Dwight and Joyce Holobaugh for surprise dinners and the YEO forum number twelve, and to Jim, Andy, Laurie, Erick, Alex, and Kelly for providing invaluable guidance throughout. Many thanks to all the contributors to this manuscript who set invested hours to share their story for the benefit of partner development managers everywhere. My gratitude to Roger for both encouragement and shouldering the responsibility of BMG so I could take the time necessary to complete the project, and, finally, to Mom, Dad and heavenly Father for making it all possible in the first place.

About the Author

SARAH GERDES is the founder and CEO of Business Marketing Group. In her twelve years in the partner development world, she has created partnerships with the world's largest, most complex, and hard-to-navigate companies, including Microsoft, Sony, Intel, and American Express.

Gerdes's breakthrough models and successful partnering techniques have been used to create more than 400 alliances and have been profiled in *Fortune*, *Inc. Magazine*, *Entrepreneur*, and *The Economist*. She has spoken to students at the top business schools in the United States, including Harvard and MIT. She is a contributing writer to a variety of business journals and an advisor to profit and non-for-profit organizations.